A History of the World Oldest Currencies Still in Use

Azhar ul Haque Sario

Copyright

First Printing, 2025

Azhar.sario@hotmail.co.uk

ORCID: https://orcid.org/0009-0004-8629-830X
Disclaimer: This book is free from AI use. The cover was designed in Microsoft Publisher

Contents

The British Pound: A Legacy of Empire, Trade, and Transformation

Think back to an era before the existence of cash or payment cards along with mobile wallets. To obtain a new axe in ancient Britain required having either a surplus sheep or the endurance to engage in intense bartering. The original trading system consisted of people trading goods and services directly with each other. Need a hand building a hut? Offer some freshly-baked bread in return. The system was straightforward but finding someone who wanted your extra cow while possessing the precise grain amount required caused significant trouble.

The "double coincidence of wants" became a significant barrier to trade. So, folks started getting smart. People discovered that items such as cattle and grain and even shiny shells were both more desirable to others and easier to trade. The first money emerged from these items which served as precursors to the modern currencies we utilize today.

The Romans arrived on the scene with their standardized coins which bore the Emperor's official image. Suddenly, trade got a whole lot smoother. Coins had established value so people stopped bartering about whether a goat was equal to a bushel of wheat. The Romans used these coins as symbols of their power rather than offering them out of pure generosity.

Chaos ensued after Roman rule ended. Due to the scarcity of coins local communities returned to bartering while regional leaders began producing their own currency. Imagine the confusion!

The arrival of the Anglo-Saxons helped restore structure to the prevailing disorder. They created mints functioning as early coin-producing factories and chose the silver penny to serve as the primary currency. The reigns of Offa and Athelstan saw them take command over coin production which guaranteed standardized quality.

The Normans maintained their tradition of order while continuing this established practice. Production standards for silver pennies were strengthened through production limits and the introduction of the "Trial of the Pyx" quality test which remains in use today in an altered form.

"Pound sterling" originated as a term describing a pound weight of pure silver. The pound sterling originated as a unit of account before it became a physical coin. During large transactions people would physically measure out silver amounts.

Over time, the system evolved. The introduction of gold coins led to a practice where monarchs secretly reduced silver content in currency to increase treasury funds which frequently resulted in inflation.

The establishment of the Bank of England in 1694 created a pivotal transformation. The introduction of banknotes signaled the start of modern banking by offering paper promises to pay specific amounts of silver or gold. The creation of paper money simplified financial transactions.

From the 20th century into the 21st century the pound sterling underwent further transformations. The United

Kingdom abandoned the gold standard which allowed the pound to float against foreign currencies while decimalization streamlined monetary operations. Our society shows a growing shift toward cashless transactions as digital payments and fintech advancements redefine money management.

So, what's next for the pound sterling? The advancement of digital currencies and financial technology along with the transition to a cashless society collectively influence the future of the pound sterling. One thing is certain: The evolution of the pound sterling from bartering systems to modern digital transactions demonstrates our ongoing adaptability and pursuit of improved trade and financial management methods.

The British pound, which the Brits fondly call "quid," tells a story more thrilling than any work of fiction. This narrative explores human ambition and power struggles while tracing the journey of the British pound through the central dynamics of an empire in conjunction with the fluctuating nature of global financial systems.

From Humble Beginnings to Imperial Might

The Anglo-Saxon period in England was defined by a trading system that depended heavily on silver pennies for economic success. The term "pound" represented more than language it symbolized concrete wealth through its equivalence to one pound of pure silver. A straightforward dependable system established the groundwork for the pound's eventual supremacy.

British merchants began their voyages with their pockets full of these silver coins that produced a jingling sound. As British merchants traveled abroad, the pound served as their universal passport while becoming a recognizable presence in busy international markets. The unwavering stability and dependability of the currency system enabled trade expansion and eliminated the difficulties associated with managing multiple currency conversions.

The British Empire's expansion marked a troubling chapter in the history of the pound. The British Empire utilized the pound as a mechanism of dominance which established an extensive "sterling area" throughout its colonies. The control Britain exercised allowed it to dominate trade and resources while managing complete economic systems.

Financing an Empire's Dreams

A successful empire requires enormous expenditures for fleets, military forces, and extensive continental infrastructure. This expansion depended on the pound which powered ambitious undertakings while establishing London as a financial superpower. The Bank of England skillfully directed the financial symphony by managing the pound with precision as it facilitated loans and investments that expanded British power across the globe.

The pound reached its highest level of influence following the 19th-century implementation of the gold standard. The pound served as the world's reserve currency which represented stability and trust during the period of fast-paced globalization. Countries used pounds as a secure fallback option to prove its consistent power.

Navigating Turbulent Waters

The 20th century unleashed numerous challenges that tested nations worldwide. The British economy suffered from two world wars which ended the pound's gold standard status and introduced instability in its value. An empire that seemed unbeatable started to collapse while the US dollar developed into a significant competitor.

The Bretton Woods system introduced after World War II established the US dollar as the dominant currency and diminished the pound sterling to a secondary role. The pound demonstrated its strength by adjusting to the floating exchange rates established in 1971 which allowed its value to align with the current state of the British economy.

The Euro Enigma and Brexit's Shockwaves

The development of the euro currency forced Britain to face a distinct choice. Britain had to decide between adopting the euro through European monetary union membership or establishing its own monetary path. Britain's choice to continue using the pound showed independence and represented its wish to direct its economic future.

Brexit emerged as a seismic event which sent shockwaves throughout the global economy. Uncertainty across the nation caused the pound to drop in value. The long-term effects of Brexit remain active in 2025 with ongoing speculation and analysis.

The Pound in the Digital Age

The pound, a veteran of countless economic battles, now faces the dawn of a new era: the rise of digital currencies. The Bank of England examines how a "digital pound" central bank digital currency (CBDC) might transform transactional methods.

The pound operates in a complex relationship with cryptocurrencies through simultaneous competitive dynamics and careful scrutiny. Although cryptocurrencies have not replaced the pound as the dominant currency, their potential to disrupt financial systems remains undeniable.

A Symbol of Strength and Identity

The pound signifies more than currency because it represents British history and national identity. The pound remains a symbol of British culture because banknotes and coins display monarchs and historical figures.

The Road Ahead

The pound's journey is far from over. The pound stands before a future that holds both major obstacles and potential benefits. The global marketplace operates with intense rivalry while technology progresses at a rapid pace and economic conditions worldwide stay consistently uncertain.

The pound will continue to thrive if the UK maintains economic stability and London stands as a leading financial center while supporting digital currency innovation.

The history of the pound demonstrates how strongly it has persisted and evolved over time. Through various challenges the pound endured changes and transformed into a representation of "Global Britain" while maintaining its influential position in the world of finance. Its future remains unwritten, but one thing is certain: The pound maintains its essential position in global affairs due to its deep historical roots and steadfast endurance.

The British pound has endured a tumultuous journey similar to a vessel facing fierce storms at sea. The British pound has endured numerous wars and economic crashes alongside political upheavals making its history a true rollercoaster ride. The government faced many difficult decisions while the pound's resilience was tested during these challenging times similar to how a ship's captain must make tough choices in dangerous waters.

The British pound has always struggled during war times. They drain resources, leaving the economy wounded. The UK faced severe financial distress during World War I which led to significant borrowing and forced abandonment of the gold standard while causing inflation to skyrocket. The currency weakened to the extent of a boxer who's cornered in the ring.

The post-war effort to restore the gold standard proved as difficult as squeezing back into pre-holiday jeans. The overvaluation of the pound resulted in expensive British exports which negatively affected the economy. World War II repeated the pattern: Massive spending alongside currency devaluation paired with strict currency exchange controls resembled a tightrope walker maintaining their precarious balance.

The currency value of the pound showed instability during smaller military conflicts such as the Falklands War. Investors become nervous when faced with uncertainty and the pound can fall dramatically much like a surfer who loses control on a large wave.

The pound has experienced difficulties during periods of economic decline. The UK permanently left the gold standard due to the devastating economic impact of the Great Depression during the 1930s. This transformation signified a complete game-changing event.

Stagflation characterized the 1970s as the economy experienced both high inflation and slow growth much like a vehicle entrenched in mud. The energy crisis worsened economic conditions which resulted in the pound's value taking a sharp dive.

The financial turmoil in 1992 that became known as "Black Wednesday" turned into a dramatic episode. The UK entered the European Exchange Rate Mechanism to achieve currency stability yet found itself defending against a besieging pound similar to a castle under attack. Speculators took positions against the currency while government efforts to protect it proved unsuccessful. The UK withdrew from the ERM while the pound underwent a significant devaluation which served as a humiliating setback.

The global financial crisis of 2008 struck like another massive earthquake. The UK banking system faced a severe disturbance and the pound suffered a dramatic fall. The UK economy worries people in the same way an unstable aircraft unsettles its passengers.

The global pandemic in 2020 triggered widespread disorder. The uncertain economic situation from lockdowns made the pound behave unpredictably as if on a rollercoaster ride in the dark.

The energy crisis drove inflation to unprecedented levels which further weakened the pound's value. The situation feels as difficult as ascending a mountain while carrying a bulky backpack.

The British pound has been significantly influenced by government policy decisions along its path. Policy decisions have the power to either strengthen or weaken the currency. The government implemented currency controls through buying and selling limitations to shield the pound from attack.

Through intentional devaluation of the pound's value governments can enhance exports while simultaneously increasing import prices. It's like a double-edged sword.

The complex history of the UK's relationship with Europe has produced numerous effects on the pound's performance. The entry into the EEC in 1973 and events including the ERM crisis, debates about adopting the euro and Brexit have all produced significant impacts.

Brexit triggered significant market volatility that hit financial markets with the force of a coastal storm surge. Following the 2016 referendum, the pound experienced a steep decline alongside mounting uncertainty about the future.

The pound has endured multiple challenges yet remains standing. This demonstrates both the enduring strength of the UK economy and its significant role throughout history. The pound continues to serve as a leading currency around the world because it remains essential for international trade and financial activities. The pound resembles a battle-hardened soldier who bears marks of past conflicts.

Global events combined with government policies and investor sentiment will influence the pound's unpredictable future. The pound will probably experience ongoing fluctuations much like a sailboat navigating uneven seas.

Multiple challenges currently face the UK economy while its global economic connections remain essential. The UK functions as a trading nation and its economic success requires international cooperation which acts like favorable winds for a ship.

The evolution of the pound shows that currency values are dynamic entities. Events continuously shape them to reflect their economic and political context. The narrative demonstrates how resilience and adaptation, along with occasional luck, play critical roles.

And the story continues to unfold. The unfolding future promises to reveal exciting developments in subsequent events. Experts predict the pound will stay strong while its long-term stability remains unknown. Government efforts are ongoing as we hope to see better times ahead. The pound represents who we are while our optimism continues unabated.

The pound's path demonstrates our ability to overcome adversities and grow stronger through difficult times. This narrative provides hope while showing that opportunities await us in the future.

Ah, the pound! It's been on a real rollercoaster ride since that fateful Brexit vote, hasn't it? Like a ship caught in a storm, it's been tossed and turned by waves of uncertainty, trade deals, and political drama. Remember that nosedive right after the referendum? Businesses were biting their nails, and investors were scrambling for life rafts.

Since then, it's been a bit of a recovery story, with the pound bravely battling its way back, though not quite to its former glory. Trade deals have been the lifebuoy, keeping it afloat, but the threat of a "no-deal" Brexit loomed like a giant kraken, ready to drag it down.

Even after the UK officially left the EU, the saga continued. The Trade and Cooperation Agreement offered a bit of a safe harbor, but it wasn't smooth sailing. Some sectors, like the fishing industry, felt like they were caught in a net of regulations.

And let's not forget the impact on people's wallets! A weaker pound means pricier imports, making everything from that morning coffee to that well-deserved holiday a bit more expensive. The Bank of England has been keeping a watchful eye on inflation, like a hawk guarding its nest.

Northern Ireland has been a particularly tricky puzzle, with the Northern Ireland Protocol adding another layer of complexity. It's like trying to navigate a ship through a narrow channel with hidden rocks.

But the pound is a fighter! It's got some powerful allies, like the UK's mighty financial services sector, new trade deals with far-off lands like the US and India, and a steady flow of foreign investment.

Looking ahead, the pound's future is still a bit of a mystery. Will it regain its former strength and become a shining beacon of stability? Or will it continue to be battered by the winds of change? Only time will tell.

But one thing's for sure, the pound is a survivor. It's weathered many storms in its long history, and it's not going down without a fight. So let's raise a glass to the pound, and wish it fair winds and following seas in the years to come!

The Serbian Dinar: Resilience Through Turmoil in the Balkans

The medieval Serbian dinar represents far more than just an ancient coin. This artifact provides insight into an intriguing historical era. The medieval Serbian dinar reveals information about political power structures and religious practices as well as commerce and the establishment and decline of a kingdom.

The coin is physical proof. The physical evidence backs the written records.

Visualize a king whose likeness has been engraved on a silver coin. The coin represents his authority as well as his right to rule and his complete control over the realm. The medieval Serbian dinar serves as a declaration of authority to his subjects and opponents while leaving a historical record that says "I am in charge."

The medieval Serbian dinar served as a powerful symbol throughout history. It's not just about buying and selling. This narrative demonstrates how a kingdom left its legacy upon the global stage.

The Nemanjić dynasty established a powerful Serbian kingdom and understood the importance of having their own currency. The Serbian government tapped into their silver mines for wealth and brought expert Saxon miners to help initiate their coin production.

The "dinar," which served as the primary Serbian currency, carries historical significance through its name. The Serbian dinar's name traces its roots back to the Roman denarius which served as a silver coin centuries before. The name dinar connects us to a powerful history while declaring our existence within a majestic lineage.

But the dinar wasn't just a copycat. The coin displayed its distinct Serbian identity through original designs and symbols. The coin depicted the leader's portrait which served as an unmistakable display of power. The coin featured religious symbols which demonstrated the strong connection between the Serbian church and state.

The dinar wasn't just for buying things. The dinar functioned as propaganda to demonstrate the Serbian kingdom's power and stability. The dinar served as a national emblem while reminding the people of their extensive history and cultural traditions.

The medieval Serbian dinar still manages to inspire people today. Designs from medieval Serbian history inspire some modern Serbian coins and banknotes which serve to honor historical legacies while keeping medieval kingdom memories alive.

The dinar serves as an emblem of Serbia's historical journey demonstrating its tenacious spirit and lasting endurance. Every small object holds the potential to reveal grand narratives.

The history of the Serbian dinar throughout Ottoman rule stands as a powerful narrative that demonstrates both the durability of a currency and the enduring spirit of the Serbian people.

A centuries-old Serbian marketplace teemed with activity as Venetian ducats and Ragusan coins mingled with Hungarian forints and Spanish reals next to Ottoman akçes in busy exchanges. Serbia's strategic location along important trade routes and its role in European economic systems are demonstrated through its history of diverse currency circulation.

While various currencies circulated through Serbian markets during medieval times as symbols of its kingdom's sovereignty, the Serbian dinar slowly disappeared from everyday trade. The Ottoman akçe, the 'dollar' of its day, steadily asserted its dominance, driven by practical realities: The Ottoman akçe dominated because merchants required a standard currency for trade while soldiers received their salaries and local taxes were collected in Ottoman money.

The elimination of the dinar represented more than economic change because it symbolized the fading pulse of the nation. The dinar's legacy persisted beyond its monetary existence through folk songs and stories which expressed a longing for the past independence.

The charismatic Karađorđe Petrović led the First Serbian Uprising in 1804 which sparked hope among the people. Despite its brief duration the rebellion resulted in the creation of new Serbian coins that featured national symbols like the cross and the letter "S" repeated four times to represent "Only Unity Saves the Serbs." The Serbian coins stood as more than money because they declared independence while showcasing the lasting Serbian spirit.

Serbia faced multiple obstacles on its path to establishing a completely independent currency system. Serbia maintained autonomy but faced complex financial management and negotiations with Ottoman authorities after gaining self-governance. The Serbian dinar was introduced in 1868 as Prince Milan Obrenović IV established its value based on the French franc to secure stability and international recognition.

The return of the Serbian dinar marked a crucial turning point which demonstrated Serbia's development into a modern independent state. The design of the currency which included Serbian rulers and national symbols strengthened the deep bond between money and Serbian national identity.

After its reestablishment the Serbian dinar has survived challenging periods which reflect the country's political and economic conditions. Despite undergoing revaluation and redesign and serving as temporary replacement during hyperinflation periods the Serbian dinar has persisted as evidence of national resilience.

The future of the Serbian dinar stays linked to Serbia's economic progress and technological development during its transition into the digital age. The emergence of digital currencies will not eliminate the Serbian dinar which serves as a physical representation of the nation's identity.

The history of the Serbian dinar demonstrates how currency serves as an emblem of national identity and sovereignty. The Serbian people demonstrated their unyielding spirit throughout their challenging journey under Ottoman control which included both loss and eventual triumph.

Envision a currency that intertwined so deeply with a nation's essence that it mirrored every success and sorrow. The Yugoslav dinar served as a monetary reflection of the nation's turbulent journey from its optimistic start to its disorderly downfall.

The Yugoslav dinar started as a symbol of national unity but ended up embodying the country's internal conflicts.

The dinar emerged from World War II's aftermath to serve as the unifying force for Yugoslavia's diverse republics. The dinar represented economic unity across a nation that spoke many languages and housed diverse cultures and histories. Though repaired like a delicate vase, its fractures remained concealed beneath the surface.

Driven by its socialist agenda the government sought to govern the dinar's future by dictating its worth forcefully. Markets naturally navigate towards their own path just as rivers flow toward their destined direction. The existence of a thriving foreign currency black market served as undeniable evidence that confidence in the dinar remained unstable like volcanic earth.

The Tito-Stalin Split: A Currency's Cold War

In 1948 Yugoslavia's Tito boldly challenged Soviet leader Stalin which dramatically changed the dinar's destiny. The split between Yugoslavia and the Soviet Union created worldwide shockwaves which the dinar felt through economic tremors. With its expulsion from the communist bloc Yugoslavia's economy became lost in an uncertain future.

The country took a distinctive route through self-management socialism which empowered workers to make decisions within factories. Although this daring experiment took place it failed to protect the dinar during the nation's search for its independent path.

The Slippery Slope to Hyperinflation

During the 1960s and 70s Yugoslavia cautiously established trade links with Western countries to attract investment. However, this economic strategy resulted in rising foreign debt. The dinar faced repeated devaluation which eroded its worth step by step.

The 1980s emerged as a decade of economic turmoil which drove the dinar to its breaking point. As the economy stumbled along, political tensions reached new heights while ethnic nationalism revealed its destructive potential. The runaway train of inflation spiraled uncontrollably into hyperinflation which acted as a monstrous vortex that stripped the dinar of its worth.

Prices doubled in days, then hours. People's life savings evaporated like morning mist. People rushed to dispose of the dinar as it turned into an undesirable burden. The government's desperate measures to stabilize the economy through new dinar issuance and decimalization of currency proved ineffective as temporary solutions for a massive financial crisis.

The Breakup: A Currency's Last Gasp

The breakup of Yugoslavia during the early 1990s marked the end of the dinar's viability as a national currency. The newly independent republics sought to establish their own currencies to demonstrate their hard-fought sovereignty. Slovenia and Croatia pioneered independence currency initiatives which others soon adopted. The dinar transformed from a symbol of unity into a relic representing a shattered dream.

The economic turmoil grew even worse when war broke out after Yugoslavia's breakup. Several currencies circulated as their exchange rates demonstrated extreme fluctuations. The period showed how political and economic disorder can create widespread confusion together with hardship.

The Dinar's Legacy: A Cautionary Tale

The history of the Yugoslav dinar teaches us that a currency represents more than its physical manifestation of paper and ink. A currency represents the essence of a nation which includes its aspirations and challenges as well as its defeats. This narrative demonstrates that political chaos combined with poor economic management reduces public confidence which results in hyperinflation and currency collapse.

The collapse of the dinar demonstrates how essential national unity and cooperation are. A nation's internal divisions result in currency vulnerability that makes it susceptible to manipulation within political conflicts. The Yugoslav dinar demonstrates through its history that economic stability requires not only a national currency but also effective governance, political stability, and public trust.

The Dinar in 2025: A Ghost of the Past

The Yugoslav dinar now stands as a historical artifact that resembles a faded photo within the pages of history. This serves as a reminder of what the nation once was before its own internal divisions caused its downfall.

The Serbian dinar and other successor currencies have developed unique stories while facing distinct hurdles. These currencies retain historical teachings because they understand that a nation's economic power directly influences its currency's strength.

The Yugoslav dinar represents a poignant legacy because its history shows ambition and hope that ended in tragedy. The tale demonstrates how a nation's currency embodies its collective soul while economic stability relies upon unity and trust supported by effective governance.

The Iraqi Dinar: The Iraqi Dinar Continues to Search for Stability While Facing Continuous Challenges in its Nation (2025 Update)

Envision a young tree sapling striving to rise above when buffeted by strong winds. The Iraqi dinar currently fights to stabilize itself amid economic and political turmoil. The Iraqi dinar reflects the tumultuous transition of Iraq as it navigates its way through a legacy of conflict and instability.

The Ghost of Hyperinflation

Iraq has been haunted by the terrifying economic monster of hyperinflation for years. A silent thief emerges at night and steals money's worth which makes people face difficulties buying basic needs while businesses face planning challenges for the future. The dinar remains trapped by hyperinflation which causes its value to fall with the force of a stone dropped from above.

Economic instability stems from war-related damages alongside heavy sanctions and fluctuating political conditions. Iraq relies on oil as its economic foundation yet faces added challenges because its price swings wildly causing further strain on the dinar.

A Currency Adrift

As of 2025 the dinar exists in a fragile state because it holds only a fraction of its previous value when measured against the robust US dollar and the consistent Euro. The Central Bank of Iraq (CBI) fights to navigate the dinar to safer financial conditions in a challenge that resembles a Herculean task.

The Central Bank of Iraq determines the official exchange rate yet the dinar's true valuation emerges from black market exchanges in busy markets. The hidden "street rate" demonstrates the actual demand for the dinar which exposes the public's mistrust in the official system and their ongoing concern about potential currency failure.

The Euro Mirage: A Tempting Oasis or a Treacherous Trap?

Leaders have proposed using the Euro as a symbol of stability and economic growth to help navigate through current financial instability. We must determine whether this potential solution stands as practical or functions as a deceptive melody that leads Iraq towards greater problems.

The allure is undeniable. The Euro aims to eliminate hyperinflation while enabling European trade and foreign investment attraction to enhance Iraq's financial standing. The concept appears as a hopeful vision that illuminates Iraq's troubled landscape.

The journey towards Euro adoption presents numerous obstacles. By adopting the Euro Iraq would lose its monetary policy autonomy and become one of the passengers in the ECB's Eurozone vehicle. The European Central Bank's policies which serve the varied Eurozone economies may not suit Iraq's specific requirements.

Iraq's oil-dependent economy reveals a sharp contrast with the Eurozone members who benefit from diversified economic activities. The Euro was created for another type of economic environment which makes it an imperfect match.

Iraq lacks the necessary economic infrastructure to meet the strict requirements needed for Eurozone membership. The national currency serves as an important symbol of Iraqi identity which makes some Iraqis reluctant to give it up.

The Dollar's Lingering Shadow

Despite not formally adopting the Euro Iraq functions under the influence of the US dollar. The "dollarization" phenomenon reveals how the dollar has become more reliable in Iraq than the dinar.

Regional Dreams: A Common Currency for the Arab World?

An additional economic dream exists alongside the euro which envisions creating a common currency for the Arab world to promote regional integration and economic cooperation. This long-term vision faces numerous challenges yet appears better suited to Iraq's economic conditions.

The Central Bank's Balancing Act

The Central Bank of Iraq keeps a delicate balance as it protects the country's financial stability. The Central Bank deploys multiple mechanisms to stabilize the dinar through interest rate adjustments alongside currency auctions and foreign currency reserve management. The Central Bank operates as if it must juggle multiple tasks while balancing on a unicycle stretched across a tightrope.

Oil's Unpredictable Dance

Oil serves as both a benefit and detriment to Iraq's economic stability while determining the future of the dinar. The value of the dinar increases when oil prices reach high levels. The dinar fails to hold its value when oil prices drop suddenly. Reliance on one commodity creates immense challenges for achieving sustained currency steadiness.

Corruption's Insidious Grip

Corruption acts like deadly venom which contaminates Iraq's economic stability and hampers the effective management of the dinar. Development funds disappear without trace which leads to reduced trust in both government operations and the currency it controls.

The Shadow Economy's Challenge

Government regulation and taxation cannot reach a substantial segment of Iraq's economy which functions in the informal sector. The existence of an "informal economy" presents challenges for governments to maintain control over the money supply and deploy successful monetary policies.

Technology's Glimmer of Hope

Mobile payment systems represent new technological opportunities which may help resolve economic issues. Such technologies enable smoother financial operations by reducing cash dependency and integrating more businesses into the formal sector which facilitates the CBI's regulatory control.

The Human Cost of Currency Instability

The economic issues at hand can overshadow the human suffering they create. Hyperinflation turns everyday life into a relentless challenge which compels families to choose between impossible options while destroying their aspirations. The constant stress combined with uncertainty negatively impacts their mental and physical health.

The Long Road Ahead

The future of the dinar remains unpredictable as its journey is filled with multiple obstacles. Quick fixes do not exist and magic wands cannot solve the problems. Iraq requires enduring solutions through comprehensive strategies that tackle the fundamental problems behind its economic difficulties.

Crucial economic reforms should both diversify the economy and decrease dependency on oil revenues. The foundation of good governance depends on both strong institutions and continuous efforts to eradicate corruption. Regional collaboration through trade partnerships and economic integration with neighboring nations delivers essential assistance.

A skilled and healthy workforce developed through education and healthcare investments is essential for enduring prosperity. All other activities depend on security stability which must take priority.

Achieving a stable dinar to represent economic prosperity and hope remains a challenging task that demands sustained effort. The Iraqi people must remain steadfast while political leaders pursue economic reforms to achieve their goal.

Although the Euro remains an unattainable vision for many, Iraq must face the daily challenge of dinar stabilization. Iraq faces a difficult journey but through determination and perseverance along with some luck it can successfully guide its currency through turbulent times toward a brighter future.

More Challenges in 2025

Re-denomination: Discussions about "re-denominating" the dinar to remove zeros from hyperinflated currency exist but fail to solve the fundamental economic issues. While this approach may make transactions easier to manage, it also runs the risk of creating confusion and diminishing trust.

Remittances: Remittances from Iraqis working abroad serve as crucial financial support by bringing foreign currency into the economy and bolstering the stability of the dinar.

US Sanctions: US sanctions against nations such as Iran produce indirect economic disturbances that affect Iraq by disrupting trade flows and weakening the dinar's value.

The Black Market's Persistence: The black market currency exchange persists through crackdown attempts because people distrust the official system.

Public Debt: Because Iraq's substantial public debt is primarily denominated in US dollars it creates additional economic complexity that demands the country keep enough foreign currency reserves.

Financial Inclusion: The majority of Iraqis live without bank access and conduct all their financial transactions with cash. Effective monetary management depends on bringing a greater number of people into the formal banking system through increased financial inclusion.

The Digital Dinar: The concept of a central bank digital currency (CBDC) which translates the dinar into digital form is becoming popular across the world. The implementation of a digital dinar might improve operational efficiency and strengthen the CBI's ability to manage money supply yet digital currency development remains nascent in Iraq.

Public Trust: Maintaining public trust stands as the fundamental element for sustaining currency stability. The public must maintain belief in the dinar and trust that its value will remain stable. The development of public trust depends on maintaining consistent policies together with transparency and stability in the political landscape.

Geopolitical Risks: The position of Iraq in a turbulent region subjects the economy to disruptive geopolitical events which affect the stability of the dinar.

A Long-Term Vision: Iraq requires an economically sound long-term economic strategy which is realistic and inclusive for its currency.

Iraq's national history mirrors the fluctuating journey of the dinar as both showcase resilience through challenges and the persistent hope for a brighter future. Despite the winding road ahead Iraq needs both determination and strategic planning along with some luck to surpass these challenges and establish a stable prosperous future for its citizens.

The Russian Ruble: A Currency of Empire, Revolution, and Resilience

Before the ruble came into existence Kievan Rus' existed as multiple principalities that each maintained its unique customs and practices. The marketplace was full of activity but instead of coins ringing together you would witness hunters trading furs for honey or craftsmen swapping tools for grain. In this economy goods functioned as money because everyone recognized their value.

Long-distance commerce required additional forms of currency beyond local barter systems. Foreign currency entered the markets with Byzantine solidi shining like gold treasure and Arab dirhams that followed the rivers as flowing silver moonlight. Far beyond mere exchange transactions these coins were concealed within the soil as future prosperity seeds reflecting the timeless human pursuit of wealth protection.

The grivna existed as an enigmatic entity cloaked in silver. Did the grivna serve as both a coin and a unit of weight? The grivna functioned like a chameleon because it altered its purpose and appearance according to the time and location. It served as a measurement for value when silver ruled as the global standard.

Kievan Rus' was ruled by powerful leaders such as Vladimir the Great who aimed to create a lasting impact on the world. They minted their own srebreniks and zlatniks which served as small silver and gold declarations of authority. These monetary experiments were brief moments of brilliance appearing in a sky filled with foreign currency influences.

The Mongol invasion emerged as a devastating storm that destroyed the existing order. The Golden Horde established itself as a massive empire which implemented both its own monetary system and unique laws. Silver began flowing again but now showed the conquerors' mark as its stamp.

Traditional practices were abolished while commerce paths changed direction as rapidly as desert sands move with the wind. Barter returned to visibility as a symbol of less complicated periods. Despite chaos life continued its course. The local lords' colors decorated the regional currencies that blossomed during this springlike period.

The small town of Moscow embarked on its journey to greatness with ambitious aspirations. The town minted coins that were rough in appearance but carried an unmistakable sense of rebellion. The proud merchant republic of Novgorod demonstrated its independence through the striking of its own silver currency. Tver and several other principalities began to participate in the monetary chaos by adding their unique voices to the new financial landscape.

The denga served as a universal currency unit across different regions while carrying its Turkic name on a small silver coin. The denga experienced instability alongside the chaotic environment as its value and weight shifted unpredictably like the ocean's tides.

The breakdown of unified systems led to the gradual formation of a new structural order. The rising star Moscow worked as a central force drawing the disparate threads of unity into one cohesive tapestry. The ruble remained an elusive goal but started forming into existence as a symbol of stability and order for a desperate nation.

A period emerged defined by transition, adjustment, and steadfast endurance. During this era monetary forms such as furs, foreign coins and local dengas became essential elements that determined the future of the nation. The period that created the foundation for modern Russia demonstrated how the human spirit overcomes adversity to create lasting progress.

The Tsarist Ruble: A Coin's-Eye View of Imperial Russia

Visualize yourself as newly minted ruble coin coming from St. Petersburg's mint. The Tsar's stern visage adorns your gleaming surface while you maintain a crisp appearance. You function not only as currency but as a minor part of an extensive imperial system while observing Russia's aspirations and challenges.

The beginning of your journey occurs when a Finance Minister examines you possibly including Sergei Witte himself. In his eyes you serve as more than mere currency because he uses you to advance Russia to become a global power. Your destiny becomes intertwined with gold which connects you to the worldwide economic system and transforms you into a representation of stability and advancement.

A Siberian railway worker's calloused hands grasp you as his sweat blends with your metallic surface. He builds railway lines through a harsh wilderness as he forges a link between Eastern and Western lands to widen the Tsar's territory. This monumental undertaking depends on you as it represents Russia's grand ambitions.

Maybe you end up in a young conscript's pocket who is destined for an unknown border. His grip on you is firm as both a symbol of his homeland and a small token for risking his life serving the Tsar. You represent both loyalty and sacrifice and serve as minor solace in an environment full of difficulties.

A Parisian salon becomes your stage as you join a loan connecting Russia and France through complicated financial and political maneuvers. Your existence represents Russia's reliance on foreign investment while you play a role in international power struggles.

But your journey isn't always glamorous. The harsh truth of factory life becomes apparent when workers labor for pitiful pay while their underlying dissatisfaction simmers beneath. A peasant clutches you desperately as he tries to pay his taxes while his livelihood hangs in the balance because of an unsympathetic regime far away.

You could become trapped amidst turbulent wartime conditions while your monetary worth rapidly declines due to rising inflation. While powerless to intervene you observe how the Tsar's diminishing authority signals an empire nearing its downfall.

The ruble serves as a tangible representation of Russia's historical achievements and setbacks alongside its aspirations and paradoxes. As a silent observer you watch history unfold becoming an insignificant thread within the vast tapestry of imperial Russia. This narrative demonstrates how powerful empires rest on unstable foundations while showing that ambition's human price manifests through minor details.

Throughout its existence, the Russian ruble experienced a volatile path characterized by revolution and war during both imperial and Soviet times.

The Russian Revolution of 1917 created a total transformation within the financial system. The ruble which had already suffered losses due to war and instability faced additional damage from the revolution. The Bolsheviks ascended to power with the objective of forming a communist state that would function through central economic planning. The Bolsheviks transformed the ruble into a key component of their economic strategy.

The initial period following the revolution experienced extreme hyperinflation coupled with widespread disorder. The Bolsheviks created massive amounts of currency to support their civil war efforts and take control of industries which resulted in the ruble becoming significantly devalued. During the economic turmoil people started exchanging goods directly and turned to foreign currencies as a means of transaction.

The New Economic Policy (NEP) started in 1921 when some private enterprises were permitted which helped restore economic stability. The introduction of a new gold-backed currency called the chervonets alongside the ruble helped restore public trust. However, this stability was short-lived.

The transition of Joseph Stalin to leadership in the late 1920s brought an end to the NEP while initiating swift industrialization and collectivization efforts. Complete government control over the economy led to a fundamental shift in the ruble's purpose. The state designated the ruble as a unit of account for its plans while removing its market value and limiting its usage to internal transactions.

The Soviet ruble remained separate from international financial networks which restricted the Soviet Union's ability to conduct foreign trade. The state of isolation resulted in the ruble losing any meaningful value in international financial markets.

The Soviet Union's disintegration in 1991 brought an end to both its centrally planned economic system and its unique currency, the Soviet ruble. As former Soviet republics gained independence they started issuing their own currencies. Russia retained the ruble designation but established an entirely new currency that was both convertible and traded internationally.

The Soviet ruble represents a distinct narrative that reveals the possibilities and restrictions of using currency as a mechanism for governmental power. The centrally planned Soviet currency system could not function effectively and resulted in economic problems due to inefficiencies and shortages while stimulating a black market and disconnecting the country from international trade.

The history of the ruble teaches crucial insights about market power and why convertibility matters while showing how currency value must match economic conditions plus highlighting isolation expenses.

Despite facing fresh obstacles the current Russian ruble functions within a market economy and shows significant differences from the Soviet-era currency. The Soviet ruble stands as a testament to the collapse of its economic system and demonstrates why currencies must be free and convertible.

The Ruble's Wild Ride: A Human Story

Imagine your life savings, the fruits of years of hard work, suddenly vanishing into thin air. This is the harsh reality that many Russians faced after the collapse of the Soviet Union in 1991. The ruble, once a symbol of stability, became a victim of the economic turmoil that followed.

The early 1990s were a time of chaos and uncertainty. Prices skyrocketed, inflation spiraled out of control, and the ruble's value plummeted. People watched in despair as their hard-earned money became worthless. The once mighty ruble was now a shadow of its former self.

The 1998 financial crisis dealt another blow to the struggling currency. The ruble collapsed, and the government defaulted on its debt. The crisis left deep scars on the Russian economy and its people.

But like a phoenix rising from the ashes, Russia slowly began to recover. Oil prices rebounded, and the government implemented reforms to stabilize the ruble. The currency regained some of its lost ground, but the memory of 1998 lingered.

In 2014, the annexation of Crimea led to Western sanctions, which further weakened the ruble. The sanctions also fueled Russia's desire to reduce its reliance on the US dollar.

Russia embarked on a journey of de-dollarization, seeking to make the ruble more independent and resilient. The country has been promoting the use of the ruble in international trade, reducing its dollar reserves, and developing alternative payment systems.

The road to de-dollarization is long and challenging. The US dollar remains the world's dominant currency, and the ruble faces many hurdles. But Russia is determined to chart its own course.

The ruble's story is not just about economics; it's about the lives of ordinary Russians. They have endured hardship and uncertainty, but they have also shown resilience and determination.

The digital ruble is a new chapter in the ruble's story. It holds the promise of faster and cheaper transactions, but it also raises questions about government control and privacy.

The ruble's future is uncertain, but one thing is clear: it is a story of survival, adaptation, and the pursuit of economic sovereignty.

The US Dollar: The Rise and Reign of a Global Reserve Currency

Picture yourself in colonial America where a marketplace buzzed with activity as it unleashed an eruption of sensory experiences. But amidst the vibrant chaos, there's a peculiar challenge: A confusing assortment of monetary systems exists that even experienced traders would find perplexing.

Picture this: In the marketplace, Spanish doubloons sounded against English shillings while French francs competed with wampum beads and beaver pelts. The marketplace operates as a financial melting pot where tobacco leaves serve as currency for ale and colorful calico fabric stands as a means to purchase shoes.

This phenomenon went beyond being a mere oddity of colonial life because it mirrored the historical context of that era. Every colony operated as an independent and self-protective entity similar to a small nation. England remained indifferent to colonial financial distress while maintaining its focus on maximizing its own treasury profits.

The result? This system triggered both frustration and fascination simultaneously. Merchants needed to perform rapid calculations to convert currencies and commodities with the expertise of an experienced accountant. The constant danger of inflation existed whereby the value of paper currency dropped faster than a runaway horse-drawn carriage.

The Revolution emerged as a fiery trial which challenged the colonies' determination and drove their financial systems to the edge. The Continental Congress, which had the responsibility to finance the military struggle, encountered substantial difficulties. Unable to raise funds through taxation the Continental Congress began printing money in excess.

The outcome was foreseeable but not completely inescapable. The value of the Continental dollar plunged as rampant inflation took hold. The phrase "Not worth a Continental" emerged frequently as people recognized the dangers of printing money without restraint.

Even as turmoil reigned supreme there remained small indications of potential redemption. Financial experts including Robert Morris used their expertise and personal wealth to bring stability to the developing country's economic system. The Constitution's adoption marked the beginning of a new period where federal authority gained the ability to establish financial order.

The establishment of the U.S. dollar represented an important milestone that symbolized national unity and economic stability. The creation of the U.S. dollar involved difficult challenges including debates over bimetallism and the emergence of state-chartered banks. The American people demonstrated resilience and creativity by successfully navigating difficulties to build a prosperous future.

The history of colonial currencies demonstrates how sophisticated and disorderly systems possess the capacity to develop and adjust. The story of human achievement demonstrates how necessity served as the driving force behind invention. Through our journey in today's financial complexities we should remember past lessons which might unlock stability and equity for everyone in the future.

Envision an era where monetary systems become combat zones for power and influence. This battle wasn't fought with physical weapons but through intellectual conflicts and power tussles that masqueraded as economic regulations. During the 19th and early 20th centuries people witnessed the perpetual transformation of money which was similar to an endless weaving process.

The gold standard served as an ancient monarch who refused to yield. His leadership style was authoritarian yet he assured the public of maintained stability and order. His strong hold became so restrictive that it threatened to suffocate the economy he aimed to safeguard. The economic pressure affected farmers and workers along with people burdened by debt. The public demanded flexibility and change in their economic system as they envisioned a young, rebellious prince to take the throne.

The greenback emerged as an audacious newcomer from the turmoil of the Civil War. The paper money existed without gold support which made it function like a wild card. Prices moved erratically because it was unpredictable. The Union's victory in the war demonstrated that money's value extended beyond physical gold.

The battle lines were drawn. Does the traditional king made of gold deserve to continue his reign? Given its many uncertainties should the greenback ascend to the throne? A conflict of principles erupted between supporters of stability and advocates for flexibility.

The forgotten prince silver remained hidden away in the tower. Many believed he held the potential to create equilibrium throughout the kingdom and distribute riches evenly. Many people worried about his influence because they thought he would disrupt the delicate power equilibrium.

The 1873 legislative act that removed silver from currency earned the label "Crime of '73." This moment became a pivotal event that launched the Populist movement. Farmers and workers chose silver as their symbol of resistance against the oppressive reign of gold. The charismatic leader William Jennings Bryan delivered his timeless "Cross of Gold" speech. The speech depicted a nation on the cross of gold while common people were sacrificed to benefit the wealthy elite.

But the old king, gold, held on. He wouldn't surrender his power so easily. The foundation for transformation had already been established. As a fresh authority to influence economic power emerged the Federal Reserve took shape. The compromise served as a bridge between traditional systems and modern changes while restoring stability to chaotic conditions.

Meanwhile, the world was watching. The strength of America increased in parallel with the growing power of its currency, the dollar. The British pound faced a new contender as the dollar started to challenge its longstanding dominance. Through world wars and economic disruptions the dollar displayed its strength and established its dominance on the global stage.

The Bretton Woods agreement functioned as a grand treaty to create a new global order following wartime turmoil. Nations around the world adopted the dollar as their primary reserve currency which marked it as the dominant currency. But even kings can fall. The decision by Nixon to disconnect the dollar from gold represented a monumental change that signified the end of previous economic regulations.

Money's narrative during this period reflects power struggles that played out within government chambers and through media channels while shaping public consciousness. Bitcoin and similar challengers have emerged today to disrupt the existing financial order in an ongoing story.

Bretton Woods and the Dollar's Rise: The narrative of Gold, Power and Shifting Sands charts the emergence of new global financial standards.

Picture this: By 1944 world war exhaustion had left international economies in ruin. The world required a new financial order to emerge from its postwar wreckage. Steaming cups of coffee accompanied tense negotiations that determined the global economic future in the quaint New Hampshire town of Bretton Woods.

A New World Order: Bretton Woods Takes Center Stage

Imagine delegates from 44 Allied nations, huddled together, their mission: The delegates aimed to establish a system designed to stop the world from experiencing another economic disaster similar to the Great Depression. The United States gained leadership status through its booming economy and extensive gold reserves while the dollar shone as a symbol of stability.

From this gathering, two powerful institutions were born: The International Monetary Fund (IMF) served as a global currency steward while the International Bank for Reconstruction and Development (IBRD) joined the World Bank to work on rebuilding and development initiatives.

The Dollar's Coronation: Long Live the King!

At the heart of Bretton Woods was a golden promise: The dollar held at a fixed rate of $35 per ounce of gold would serve as the foundation for the entire global economy. The dollar served as the standard reference point for all other currencies to maintain fixed exchange rates. The economic framework functioned on mutual trust and positioned the dollar at its central point of brilliance.

The "gold-dollar standard" generated a period of exceptional economic development and stable growth. The dollar took on the role of global reserve currency and became essential for international trade while representing American economic power.

Cracks in the Facade: The Dollar's Golden Armor Starts to Tarnish

The dollar's dominance encountered obstacles similar to those faced by any great kingdom. America's gold reserves diminished because of its spending on the Vietnam War alongside foreign aid programs and investments abroad. Doubts crept in. Would it prove feasible for the U.S. to sustain its golden commitment? Countries started trading their dollars for gold which created extreme strain on the economic system.

The Nixon Shock: A King's Gambit

Then came the bombshell. In 1971, President Nixon, facing a dwindling gold supply, made a dramatic decision: he severed the dollar's link to gold. The "Nixon Shock" created global economic turmoil by dismantling the Bretton Woods system and initiating the use of floating exchange rates.

A World Adrift: Navigating the Floating Seas

The world found itself navigating through waves of unpredictability. Currencies fluctuated, creating both risks and opportunities. Although experts anticipated the collapse of the dollar it demonstrated greater strength than they expected.

The Dollar's Enduring Reign: Why the King Still Wears the Crown

The United States economy's vast scale and continuous growth propelled the dollar to maintain its dominant position. The dollar continued to serve as the preferred medium for global trade and investment activities because of its established position within the worldwide financial infrastructure.

As the world's reserve currency the U.S. gained tremendous power including cheap borrowing capabilities and deficit running options while maintaining influence through sanctions.

The Gathering Storm: Challenges to the Dollar's Throne

But the dollar's reign is not unchallenged. China's growing global influence prompts its efforts to extend the international use of its currency called the yuan. Emerging technologies such as cryptocurrencies and central bank digital currencies (CBDCs) have the potential to disrupt the established financial order.

The United States' expanding national debt together with its dependency on sanctions as an instrument for policy makes many people anxious. Various countries are exploring alternative currencies to minimize their reliance on the U.S.-dominated financial structure.

Will the dollar remain dominant or will we enter an era of multiple currencies?

The dollar's future is uncertain. The dollar will probably not lose its status quickly but a progressive move toward multiple currencies appears feasible. A more fragmented financial landscape could result from the development of other economies combined with new technological advances and geopolitical transformations.

The Legacy of Bretton Woods: A World in Constant Flux

The small town of Bretton Woods in New Hampshire contributed significantly to the formation of the post-war economic structure. The period was marked by the emergence of the dollar as the dominant world currency. As global dynamics transform the world evolves and so does the future of the dollar along with the ever-changing global economy. The monetary narrative continues to unfold with promise for future chapters that will match previous ones in excitement.

The Greenback: Still Top Dog, But Feeling the Bite?

Picture the US dollar as a veteran boxer who has maintained the championship title for many years. The Greenback has faced multiple battles and interruptions yet maintains its position as the dominant currency. New contenders are stepping into the boxing ring who are younger and quicker while they seek to snatch the reigning champion's title.

What historical events led to the US dollar becoming the dominant global currency?

Think back to the dollar's glory days. How did it rise to the top?

America's Economic Knockout: The US economy emerged as a global powerhouse following World War II. American goods required dollars for purchase by people globally.

The Bretton Woods Pact: The Bretton Woods Pact established a system where numerous world currencies were tied to the US dollar which itself was pegged to gold until that linkage was eventually severed.
Oil's Dollar Dance: The majority of oil transactions are conducted in U.S. dollars through what is known as the petrodollar system. This keeps demand for the dollar high.
Trust and Stability: Investors viewed the US as the safest investment option. The public maintained confidence that the dollar would retain its stability and not face rapid devaluation.
Network Effect Power-Up: The dollar gained functionality as more people started using it. The US dollar functions as a sought-after membership card because its popularity attracts everyone.
Deep Pockets and Fair Play: The United States maintains an extensive financial market that operates openly under strict regulatory standards.
Military Muscle: A robust military capability helps maintain economic stability.

The Dollar maintains its status as the dominant global reserve currency in early 2025.

At present, the dollar maintains its status as the dominant global reserve currency. This means:

Central Banks' Piggy Bank: Countries maintain dollar reserves which serve as a worldwide emergency fund.

International Trade's Common Tongue: Dollars function as the standard currency for pricing international trade goods and services.
Debt's Dollar Denominator: Nations and businesses frequently choose to take out loans denominated in dollars.

The atmosphere suggests that transformations are imminent. Whispers of doubt, new challengers approaching. The dollar's supremacy appears to be slipping.

Challengers to the Throne

A variety of elements contribute to the unpredictable future of the dollar.

The Dragon's Ascent (and its Yuan):

The Chinese economy stands as the world's second most extensive national economy. China wants its currency the yuan (renminbi) to become more influential internationally.

Trading in Yuan: Through agreements with nations including Russia and Brazil as well as several African countries China promotes the usage of yuan for trade.
Digital Yuan: The digital currency e-CNY positions China ahead of other nations by simplifying the process for external countries to adopt its system.
"Belt and Road" Expansion: Through this extensive infrastructure initiative China strengthens its global position while creating opportunities for increased use of the yuan.

The Euro's Staying Power:

The euro serves as the second most widely held reserve currency by nations around the world. The euro remains second to the dollar yet continues to show strong potential as a reserve currency.

Economic Heavyweight: The EU is a major economic force.
Internal Challenges: The Eurozone has experienced multiple issues such as the Greek debt crisis which has occasionally undermined trust in the euro.

The Crypto Craze (and its Wild Card):

Bitcoin and Ethereum along with other digital currencies are creating significant disruptions. They're not controlled by any government.

Decentralized Dance: This is their main appeal. Theoretically speaking, no central bank has control over cryptocurrency operations.
Volatility Rollercoaster: The wild price swings of cryptocurrencies make them unsuitable as stable reserve currencies.
Regulation on the Horizon: The initiation of cryptocurrency regulation by governments may reduce its appeal to certain investors but promises to enhance overall stability.
Stablecoins: These dollar-pegged cryptocurrencies function as a potential link between traditional finance and digital financial systems.

Globalization's Double-Edged Sword:

While the dollar became dominant due to globalization it now faces increased competition from other currencies.
More Trade, More Choices: International trade between countries is increasing beyond the US which allows more currencies to enter global markets.
Shifting Power Dynamics: The distribution of global power remains unsettled and is undergoing transition. While the

United States remains powerful, other nations are beginning to emerge as significant players.

US Debt and Spending Habits:

The United States carries a massive debt burden which leads some observers to believe that it could diminish the dollar's value in the future.

Spending Spree and IOUs: The US government operates with high expenditures which it offsets through borrowing.
Inflation Fears: Printing excessive money by the government to settle debts can lead to inflation which will reduce the dollar's value.

Trust is Key: When the US economy loses investor confidence they will likely search for alternative investment opportunities.

Sanctions and the Dollar's Weaponization:

The United States has exercised its control over the dollar to enforce economic sanctions against countries such as Russia and Iran.

Seeking Alternatives: Countries that depend on this system are actively seeking alternative solutions.

Digital Currencies from Central Banks (CBDCs):

Central banks are working on creating their own digital currencies.

Potential Game-Changer: The development of CBDCs has the potential to create major changes in the structure of international finance.

A World with Many Money Kings?

What will these changes imply for our future financial systems? One possibility is a multipolar currency system.

Sharing the Throne: Multiple currencies might work together to share global financial dominance instead of the dollar reigning alone.
The Yuan, the Euro, and Others: These would be the main contenders.
Currency Cliques: Currency blocs could develop where Asian nations adopt the yuan as their primary currency while European countries maintain their use of the euro.
Complexity and Resilience: The international financial system would gain resilience while becoming more complex because it would distribute currency reliance across multiple countries.

The Digital Wild Card

Digital currencies are a game-changer.

Central Bank Digital Currencies (CBDCs): Numerous countries including the United States are investigating CBDCs which represent digital versions of their current national currencies.

Competition or Collaboration? : CBDCs might challenge the dollar or become a part of the current financial framework. It's too early to tell.
Privacy Concerns: Concerns exist about privacy because the implementation of CBDCs may enable governments to monitor all financial transactions.

The Dollar's Still Got It

The dollar maintains significant advantages despite these challenges:

Force of Habit: The existing system has been around for such a long time that changing it proves very difficult. Everyone is used to the dollar.
Financial Heavyweight: The US financial system remains the largest and most advanced worldwide.
Military Might: The US military continues to be the strongest force which delivers security and stability.

Law and Order: The United States possesses a robust legal system which enhances its safety for investment.

Looking Into the Future (2030 and Beyond).

Forecasting what lies ahead proves difficult though we can suggest some possible outcomes:

Dollar Still Strong, But Sharing the Stage: The dollar will retain its status as a key reserve currency but may lose ground in global reserve holdings.

Yuan's Rising Star: China will maintain its efforts to expand the global use of the yuan.

Digital Currency Boom: Central bank digital currencies along with select cryptocurrencies will achieve broader mainstream adoption.
Currency Rollercoaster: Currency relationships could show increased volatility in the future.
Gradual Shift: The dollar's dominance won't disappear overnight.

The Human Side of Money

This isn't just about numbers and graphs. It's about people.

Jobs: A declining value of the dollar could create job impacts in the United States particularly within industries that rely heavily on exporting goods.
Travel: Americans might pay more or less for international travel as the dollar experiences fluctuations.
Global Power Plays: America's global influence determines the strength of the dollar's status. The diminishing dominance of the dollar indicates potential changes in global power structures.
Confidence: The dollar represents American economic power and stability beyond its basic function as currency.

The Bottom Line

The dollar is facing real challenges. China's growth together with the euro currency and digital financial assets alongside US debt worries threatens to challenge the dollar's dominance. The world might soon operate under a system where multiple currencies share global dominance. The dollar maintains its power and will remain relevant for the foreseeable future. Upcoming years will play a decisive role in determining the trajectory of the dollar and the structure of the global financial system. We are witnessing change and it promises to be an incredible show. The King has not passed away yet though his control appears to be weakening.

The Haitian Gourde: A Currency of Struggle and Survival

The Haitian Gourde serves as a monetary reflection of Haiti's national challenges.

The Haitian gourde came into existence through revolutionary strife and reflects the tumultuous path of its people. The history of the gourde from colonial times to its present-day economic difficulties represents a consistent narrative of endurance and adaptation while pursuing self-sustained economic autonomy.

French Colonialism: Seeds of Discontent

The French Empire relied heavily on their colony Saint-Domingue for financial profits before Haiti gained independence. The flow of French livres, sous, and deniers through the hands of enslaved Africans served as a powerful symbol of colonial dominance.

The monetary system functioned as a tool to uphold French control over the colony. The system allowed trade between the colony and France but kept all the generated riches under French control. The enslaved people experienced growing resentment towards their economic oppression since the system represented their complete subjugation.

Revolution and Monetary Chaos

The Haitian Revolution signaled hope to enslaved people worldwide and disrupted the colonial structure while causing monetary disorder. The war created monetary chaos with multiple currencies in circulation including

French colonial money and Spanish coins along with temporary revolutionary currencies.

The production of weapons consumed metal supplies which intensified monetary system disruptions. Paper money that lacked proper backing rapidly lost value leading to inflation and loss of public trust. The financial disruption reflected the wider fight to achieve both political freedom and economic self-sufficiency.

Early Independence: A Quest for Stability

After the revolution concluded Haiti had to confront the difficult challenge of creating a new monetary system. The establishment of a new monetary system served dual purposes by ensuring economic stability while confirming the sovereignty of Haiti as an independent nation.

The initial effort to make coffee beans serve as money demonstrated practical difficulties. The paper money system fell into failure since the distribution of land as collateral proceeded slowly and involved many disputes. In 1813 Haiti introduced the gourde which took its name from a Spanish silver coin to replace the colonial livre.

The Gourde: A Symbol of Hope and Resilience

The gourde stood for more than monetary value because it represented Haitian independence and marked the nation's transition from colonial rule to sovereign statehood. The initial gourdes were silver coins featuring national symbols which helped build a sense of unity and identity.

The initial years of the gourde's circulation faced numerous difficulties. The revolution left Haiti's economy in ruins while the country endured global isolation. The large indemnity demanded by France placed additional strain on Haiti's economy which restricted the government from making developmental investments.

The Gourde's Turbulent Journey

The value of the gourde experienced multiple fluctuations throughout the 19th and 20th centuries as it mirrored Haiti's persistent economic and political difficulties. During the early 20th century US occupation Haiti the gourde became pegged to the US dollar which provided stability while taking away Haiti's control over its monetary policy.

The gourde faces ongoing challenges such as inflation and political instability as well as natural disasters throughout the 21st century. The Haitian Central Bank's attempts to stabilize the currency have failed as the gourde continues to depreciate against the US dollar and thus diminishes Haitian citizens' buying power.

The Gourde: More Than Just Money

The gourde stands as a timeless emblem of Haitian cultural identity and national endurance despite its economic challenges. The gourde stands as a testament to Haitian independence and their continued pursuit of economic stability and prosperity.

The historical importance of the gourde cannot be disputed despite its unclear future. The gourde stands as both a physical connection to Haiti's history and a declaration of its national story while offering hope for what lies ahead.

The Haitian gourde operates like a ship lost in a storm continuously battered by unforgiving waves. Haiti's currency functions as both a mirror of its national identity and an indicator of its ongoing challenges. A tiny overloaded boat with leaks struggles to find its way through a raging hurricane. That's the gourde.

1. The Political Maelstrom:

Haiti's political situation resembles a volcano ready to erupt at any moment. Political turmoil emerges from coups and fraudulent elections as leaders maintain their hold on power like stubborn barnacles on a ship's hull which creates disastrous conditions. Successive presidents lead Haiti with their own economic strategies which send the gourde into rapid, unpredictable turns.

Corruption functions as a destructive termite that continuously eats through the economic structure. Every stolen dollar combined with every shady transaction gradually reduces the gourde's value. The situation resembles pouring water into a bathtub that has a huge hole in its base.

The streets are dominated by gang violence while kidnapping has emerged as a dark industrial sector. Operating a business in such turbulent conditions is comparable to working in a war zone. Any investor would avoid putting money into a location that presents danger at every turn.

2. Shackled by Dependence:

Haiti's economy functions like a fledgling bird that lacks the ability to take flight independently. The Haitian economy requires US dollars to purchase essential imports because it lacks the ability to produce its own currency. It feels as if you're endlessly thirsty in the desert while carrying just a tiny canteen.

Money sent back to Haiti from expatriates serves as an essential financial lifeline with valuable dollars reaching the nation. The existence of Haiti remains fragile because it depends on the success of other nations. Visualize a household whose stability depends entirely on financial support from a relative while lacking full security in their home.

Foreign aid serves important purposes yet it presents serious challenges. This crutch enables walking yet stops you from building your own strength. The requirements set by donors act as constraints which hinder Haiti's ability to determine its own path forward.

3. Nature's Fury:

The beauty of Haiti stands alongside its tragic susceptibility to disaster. Earthquakes along with hurricanes and floods unleash destruction reminiscent of biblical plagues as they devastate everything around them. Every year floods sweep away a farmer's crops and carry his dreams away with the water.

These disasters function as economic shocks which cause the gourde to plummet. Haiti must borrow funds when rebuilding after disasters which leads to a growing debt burden that puts heavy strain on its currency.

4. The Weight of Intervention:

Haiti has endured a lengthy period of foreign intervention which provided both assistance and obstacles. Throughout history the US and France along with various international organizations have acted both as protectors and troublemakers for Haiti. Envision an affectionate relative who means well but frequently gives advice without fully grasping your personal circumstances.

Humanitarian aid packages provide critical help yet frequently carry attached requirements which generate controversy and potential harm. The gift comes with undisclosed requirements.

The Long Road to Stability:

The process of stabilizing the gourde resembles a mountain ascent because it demands sustained effort without any shortcuts. To achieve success it needs a complete overhaul along with reconstruction from its base.

Envision Haiti as a critically ill patient who requires immediate medical attention. Haiti's economy requires diversification which functions like how a body enhances its immune system. Haiti must channel funds into education and healthcare to nurture both mental and physical well-being. Governance must be reinforced through decisive action just as a fractured bone requires proper treatment. The nation must enhance its disaster preparedness capabilities through actions such as constructing storm shelters.

The fundamental task requires building trust which is essential just like a doctor who instills confidence in their patient. The Haitian people should place their trust in their national currency while believing in their own future prospects. Although the toughest task Haiti faces stands before it, this challenge remains essential for realizing the nation's full potential.

Though the path forward presents many challenges the Haitian people demonstrate great strength. They have survived many turbulent times and they will keep pushing towards a better tomorrow where the gourde represents power rather than hardship.

The intense sun shines brightly over Port-au-Prince's active marketplace. Marie focuses intently while arranging her mangoes on the dusty ground where their bright colors stand out vividly. Through years of experience she has mastered mental calculations that enable her to remember the price of each item instinctively. She keeps her ragged Gourdes from work secure as proof of her dedication. Marie understands how inflation slowly devours her small income resulting in diminishing finances each day.

In the market Jean-Baptiste spends his time working on a motorcycle engine while his calloused hands and determined eyes show his determination. His expertise as a mechanic stems from years of repairing any vehicle that has wheels. A farmer who needs repairs for his broken-down truck presents Jean-Baptiste with a sack of yams as payment for his services today. This system isn't perfect but represents everyday functioning in a world where formal economic structures remain an unreachable dream.

Madame Dubois in a mountain village sorts through the bright money she earned from selling her woven baskets with the careful touch of someone who learned the value of years. This currency called "Soleil" serves as a local financial system which people created to avoid the unstable national money while promoting self-sufficiency. This venture carries high risks yet offers potential for an improved tomorrow.

The informal economy of Haiti showcases individuals who rely on resourcefulness and resilience to survive. The official currency Gourde faces difficulties in matching the practical demands of everyday life. The decreasing value of money because of inflation pushes people to develop innovative methods to safeguard their earned income. People desire dollars yet they remain inaccessible for minor purchases. The time-tested practice of barter is experiencing a resurgence that establishes direct physical connections between people.

The promise of convenience and accessibility from mobile money delivers a small ray of hope. Reliable networks are still inconsistent and trust remains unestablished. Despite ongoing efforts to integrate all individuals into formal financial systems, financial inclusion remains an unmet objective. The substantial influence of microfinance institutions through their small loans provides essential support to many people yet fails to serve everyone.

As experimental financial systems Soleil and Bitcoin stand out by opposing established monetary systems while giving communities increased power. They present dangers such as market volatility and unpredictable regulations.

The future of Haiti's informal economy is uncertain, but one thing is clear: The Haitian people will persist in finding ways to succeed because their entrepreneurial spirit remains steadfast. The Haitian people maintain the economy's foundation while powering innovation and protecting traditions. The stories that intertwine with everyday life affirm the lasting power of the human spirit.

The Gourde's Future: Can Monetary Policy Really Help Haiti?

Haiti possesses a dynamic culture and strong population yet remains burdened by enduring challenges. The shadow of poverty extends far into society while inequality remains a harsh fact of life. The Gourde represents Haiti's nation's hope and uncertainty while the country continues to face its numerous challenges. Does Haiti's management of its monetary policy have the power to create significant change?

Navigating the Monetary Maze

Think of money's movement like a river with the Banque de la République d'Haïti (BRH) serving as its protector. The BRH works to maintain the smooth flow of the river while avoiding both inflationary rapids and recessionary droughts. Their tools? Interest rates function as dams that control the river's flow while the money supply acts like rain which replenishes the river.

A Glimmer of Hope: Monetary Policy's Potential

A well-functioning economic system relies on stable prices as its fundamental support structure. The surge in prices leads to financial difficulties for families and business failures while spreading general uncertainty. Inflation represents the most dangerous economic threat while effective monetary policy stands as its strongest defense. Low interest rates operate as nurturing rain which prompts business investment and expansion through job creation and opportunity generation. Foreign investors may be drawn to Haiti because a stable Gourde brings essential capital to the country.

The Weight of Reality: Poverty and Inequality

The root of Haiti's problems extends to profound depths similar to earth fissures. Monetary policy alone cannot mend them. The burden of poverty holds down millions of people making economic advancement difficult for them. The wide economic gap between wealthy individuals and impoverished citizens creates additional challenges. Without borrowing options people find lower interest rates to remain unattainable dreams.

The Haitian Landscape: A Complex Tapestry

Agriculture together with international remittances and frequent natural disasters combine to form Haiti's economic tapestry. Progress suffers from both natural disasters like earthquakes and hurricanes and political instability's shadow that breeds uncertainty. The BRH has the responsibility to navigate the economy but encounters interference which disrupts its ability to maintain a steady economic direction.

A Vision for 2025: Seeds of Change

Although we cannot predict what the future holds, we should have the courage to envision our dreams. Envision a 2025 where the BRH has successfully reduced inflation and created stability for regular Haitian people. Visualize programs that support small businesses by offering credit access and promoting innovative growth. Visualize government investments in infrastructure such as roads and essential utilities including electricity and water that maintain a thriving economy.

Financial Inclusion: Bridging the Gap

The integration of Haitians into formal banking systems functions as a bridge over economic separations. Bank accounts enable families to store their savings securely while providing access to loans which allows full economic participation. Mobile banking operates as a beacon of hope and extends financial services to remote regions empowering marginalized communities.

The aspiration for regional unity remains far from reality.

Regional financial unity through a Caribbean currency similar to Europe's Euro remains an unspoken dream in the region. The vision represents unity through improved trade systems and lowered risks. The journey ahead remains extensive and filled with numerous obstacles. Haiti's distinct and sensitive economy requires alignment with neighboring countries which involves substantial reforms and consistent commitment.

Cooperation, Not Integration: A More Realistic Path

Complete currency integration continues to exist as an unattainable goal at this point. Caribbean nations can achieve closer collaboration through strategic initiatives. A collaboration that encourages knowledge sharing and coordinated anti-financial crime efforts combined with strengthened regulations will lead to a more stable and prosperous region.

The Pillars of Progress: A Holistic Approach

Monetary policy serves as a single element among many essential tools in development. Education investment alongside workforce development functions as planting seeds which will grow into a brighter future. A healthy population created by improved healthcare functions as an optimal environment for growth. Building strong governance and eliminating corruption serves as a fundamental foundation for future success.

Empowering Women: The Ripple Effect

The empowerment of women represents an essential economic necessity beyond achieving justice. When women thrive, communities prosper. Entrepreneurial support programs that offer women access to credit and training create waves of beneficial change.

The Land's Bounty: Supporting Agriculture

The agricultural sector which serves as Haiti's economic foundation requires steadfast support. By equipping farmers with improved seeds alongside advanced technology and irrigation systems yields will grow stronger and more reliable. Improved infrastructure that connects farmers to markets will reveal their full potential.

The Diaspora's Embrace: More Than Just Remittances

Haitians who live outside their country function as an essential lifeline through their remittance contributions to their families' survival. Their impact extends beyond monetary aid to provide broader support. Haitians living abroad have the potential to invest in businesses while sharing their skills and serving as links between Haiti and the global community. Promoting diaspora investments through incentives can stimulate economic development and generate new opportunities.

Building Resilience: Weathering the Storms

The country of Haiti requires an active strategy to handle its susceptibility to natural disasters. Communities can endure storms and rebuild with increased strength through early warning system investments and stronger building codes alongside disaster relief funds establishment.

The Human Face of Economics

Graphs and policies often overshadow the real human stories that matter. Every number represents a family's experience along with their hopes and battles. Monetary policy functions as a strategic instrument to enhance living conditions while creating better opportunities and developing a fair and just society.

A Long Road Ahead: Hope Endures

Despite daunting challenges Haiti continues to demonstrate its historical resilience. Its people are strong, its culture vibrant. Sound policies combined with international support and sustainable development practices enable progress. Monetary policy serves as a guiding light but lacks the power of a magical solution. The strategy needs to put people first while empowering them and creating a brighter future through healing for Haiti.

The Falkland Islands Pound: A Currency of Isolation and Contested Sovereignty

A windswept archipelago exists in the distant South Atlantic where more penguins than people live and historical echoes spread throughout the rugged terrain. The Falkland Islands reveal their history and people through their currency which symbolizes identity and endurance while connecting them to distant origins.

The islanders maintained an ancient barter system before the Falkland Islands pound introduced crisp banknotes and coins to their economy. Ships arrived with potatoes while locals traded sheep to obtain the same, an old fishing net could earn a warm coat through direct trade. When British settlers migrated to these shores during the 19th century the familiar pound sterling started appearing in people's pockets and purses.

The remote islands that lay nearer to Antarctica than to London confronted an essential problem. Securing a regular flow of British money was as impossible as capturing snowflakes during a storm. The Falkland Islands began producing their own banknotes in 1899 because they needed to address logistical issues while asserting their independence. These banknotes went beyond their monetary function to represent a community's commitment to self-definition and settlement establishment.

The Falkland Islands pound serves as a proud symbol that represents the distinct identity of this community. While being tied to the British pound sterling this currency illustrates the strong relationship between the islands and Britain and demonstrates the unique identity of the Falkland Islands. The flip of a Falkland Islands coin reveals either a playful penguin, a majestic Black-browed albatross or a sturdy sheep which serve as reminders of the natural beauty influencing island life.

This currency serves a dual purpose as both a means of exchange and a fundamental element that binds the islands' social identity. The local currency serves as a concrete connection to British roots for the Falkland Islanders while functioning as an emblem of their self-rule and a silent challenge to Argentina's territorial claims.

The Falkland Islands pound stands out as a delightful exception in today's era of globalized financial systems and digital payments. Money serves multiple roles beyond trade as it represents a people's voice while also acting as both their historical record and symbol of their lasting spirit. The next time you walk along these windy beaches make sure to reflect on the tale that the money in your possession reveals about this distant archipelago and its enduring people and their distinctive place in the world.

The Falklands War created economic challenges for the islands which they managed to overcome.

The intense and brief Falklands War of 1982 transformed the Falkland Islands' economic structure. The Falklands War extended beyond political and military dimensions. The conflict led to significant economic changes for the islands including their monetary system and their financial reliance on the UK along with alterations to their currency's symbolic meaning.

Before the Storm: A Precarious Economy

The Falklands' economy existed in a vulnerable state prior to 1982. The economy depended heavily on sheep farming and wool exports. The population was small.

Investment was limited. There wasn't much economic diversification. The islands displayed numerous economic weaknesses across different sectors.

The War's Immediate Economic Shock

The Argentine invasion started economic turmoil in April 1982. Normal life stopped. Farming was severely affected. Businesses closed. The islands experienced infrastructure damage due to the warfare. Supply chains were cut off. The economy basically ground to a halt.

The Pound as a Symbol of Defiance

Argentina attempted to force the use of the Argentine peso throughout their occupation. They wanted to erase British influence. But the Falkland Islanders resisted. The Falkland Islanders retained the Falkland Islands pound which remains directly tied to the British pound sterling. The use of their own currency and British money emerged as a strong act of defiance from the Falkland Islanders. It showed their loyalty to the UK. It was a rejection of Argentine rule. The resistance represented a silent yet powerful opposition.

Post-War: Increased British Financial Support

Following the war the United Kingdom increased its financial support drastically. The islands needed help to rebuild. The war had exposed their economic vulnerability. The UK government recognized this. The UK government recognized a need to make financial investments in the future of the islands.

Rebuilding and Reconstruction Aid

After the conflict ended massive financial support poured into the Falklands from Britain. This money was used for several things. Houses had to be rebuilt. Roads needed repair. The airport was expanded. New infrastructure projects were started. The goal was to mend the destruction from the war while helping the economy to grow.
The British government spent substantial funds to bring public services back to full functionality.

Diversification Efforts: Beyond Sheep

The war demonstrated how risky it is to depend on just one industry for economic stability. The Falklands government together with the UK began researching economic diversification strategies. This was a long-term goal. The main goal was to enhance the islands' resilience.

Fishing Takes Center Stage

The fishing industry experienced major development which became one of the largest changes in the region. The Falklands established a 150-mile fishing territory around their islands in 1986. The original 150-mile fishing zone expanded to cover 200 miles later on. The declaration of a fishing zone around the Falkland Islands provided them control over extensive fishing resources. Foreign fleets' purchase of fishing licenses became the islands' principal revenue stream. It transformed the islands' finances.

Tourism: A Growing Sector

Initially tourism showed gradual growth on the islands. The conflict attracted attention as a point of interest. Battlefield tours began to attract visitors. Wildlife unique to the islands like penguins attracted many tourists. The Falklands joined the routes of cruise ships for their tours.

Military Spending: A Constant Presence

After the conflict ended the UK continued to have a substantial military deployment on the islands. The military presence served defensive purposes and simultaneously boosted the local economy. The stationed military members used their money to support businesses throughout the local economy. The development and upkeep of military installations resulted in employment opportunities.

The Falkland Islands Pound: Still Standing Strong

The official currency of the Falkland Islands continues to be the Falkland Islands pound. The Falkland Islands pound continues to maintain its fixed exchange rate with the British pound sterling. This link provides stability. The currency link maintains and strengthens the Falkland Islands' relationship with the United Kingdom. The Argentine government maintains its challenge to the sovereignty of the islands. The pound functions as an unending symbol of the islands' British heritage.

Challenges and Uncertainties

Despite the economic progress, challenges remain. The islands are still geographically isolated. This makes trade and transportation more expensive. The islands struggle with workforce limitations because of their small population size. There are ongoing tensions with Argentina.

The Argentine Factor

The persistent territorial claims of Argentina result in economic instability for the islands. Argentina has occasionally attempted to control access to the islands by restricting trade. They have demonstrated opposition to the exploitation of fishing resources. These measures contribute additional challenges to the Falklands' economic condition.

Brexit's Potential Impact

Brexit resulted in the United Kingdom facing unexpected uncertainties as it separated from the European Union. The Falklands used to gain access to EU markets. New trade agreements had to be negotiated. Economists continue to evaluate how Brexit will affect the islands' economy over time.

Oil Exploration: A Potential Game-Changer?

Oil and gas exploration continues in the waters surrounding the Falklands. The discovery and exploitation of significant reserves would radically transform the Falklands' economic landscape. However, this is a controversial issue. Argentina strongly objects to any oil exploration.

The Future: Sustainability and Self-Sufficiency

The Falkland Islands government prioritizes sustainable development in their economic planning. Their goal is to sustain economic growth while protecting environmental health. They also aim to increase their self-sufficiency. Their goal is to decrease dependency on foreign assistance.

A Resilient Economy

The Falklands War was a turning point. The war pushed the islands to face their economic weaknesses. The outcome was an increased need for British assistance. But it also spurred diversification and growth. The current economy demonstrates greater resilience compared to its state before 1982.

In Stanley the gusty wind transports saline air together with an unidentified earthy aroma. "Listen to those sheep!" Sarah chuckles while her fifth-generation islander cheeks flush from the chilly air. "Can't escape it, can you? The sea runs through our veins as naturally as our blood flows through our bodies. On Ross Road Sarah operates a small shop that offers hand-knitted wool sweaters together with penguin-themed souvenirs. "Tourists really love them," she adds with a wink, "and they help pay the bills when fishing isn't bringing in much."

In the Falklands, the Falklands Pound represents more than simple currency. This currency functions as a fundamental part of life across the remote archipelago demonstrating resilience together with a connection to the distant homeland. Through its existence the Falklands Pound illustrates the islands' distinctive economic challenges while navigating the rough waters of worldwide financial systems.

Sheep continue to roam the wind-swept hills of the Falklands as they once ruled the land while their wool serves as a connection to the past. The weathered face of Old man Davies recalls an era when wool dominated the economy. "You would have been able to purchase a house after one successful shearing," he tells me with his voice showing signs of aging. Farmers remain anxious because wool prices now respond to global market trends making their livelihoods uncertain.

The real action takes place at sea. The vibrant fishing vessels return to Stanley harbor with squid and fish that sustain the Falklands economy. Fishing is tough work but runs in his veins like sheep farming runs in old Davies' blood, says young Tom with his weathered hands and playful eyes. The value of the Falklands Pound moves according to the fluctuations in the fishing industry as it depends on established quotas and changing tastes of overseas buyers.

The currency stabilization provided by its link to the British Pound stands as a crucial connection to Britain. The UK economy functions like a rollercoaster ride whose volatility affects these remote islands deeply. Sarah lets out a sigh and shakes her head as she says, "Brexit was a serious setback. The markets now present more obstacles for our fish exports.

Argentina remains a threatening presence on the distant skyline. The ongoing sovereignty dispute continues to create an unresolved wound that darkens the islands' future prospects. "They want to suppress us," Sarah declares firmly, "but we won't let them dominate us." Our people possess the same stubborn strength as the resilient gorse that grows on these hills.

The Falklands Pound stands as a defiant symbol and a clear statement of self-determination. Underneath these waves they claim oil exists which could transform the situation entirely. Engaging in this venture poses significant risks which might reignite past conflicts. The islanders have developed a familiarity with taking risks. The people here have built their existence within this rugged yet stunning land as proof of their resilient nature.

A young girl stands on the cliffs as the sky above Stanley takes on pink and gold shades during sunset while the wind blows through her hair. The vast ocean before her evokes both fear and optimism in her gaze. The future of the Falklands Pound, like the future of the islands themselves, is uncertain, but one thing is for sure: These islanders demonstrate toughness and resourcefulness which will continue to survive.

The Dominican Peso: A Currency of Resilience and Transformation in the Caribbean

A fledgling nation emerges from the battle for independence as it searches for its place in the world. It resembles a fledgling that has been pushed out of its nest and now struggles with unstable wingbeats despite exerting maximum effort. The Dominican Republic and its peso currency experienced a prolonged and complex journey to achieve financial stability.

It started off as a bustling marketplace with people shouting across the space. People carried a mix of Spanish reales and Haitian gourdes among other unknown coins that caused a strange musical jingle in their pockets. The nation that had just gained independence sought to establish financial control by stating "We need our own currency." The first attempts by the country to establish their currency appeared successful initially but ended up failing like an inexperienced baker's failed souffle.

The franco entered the scene as a refined European presence who attempted to introduce order to the chaotic gathering. The franco acted as a school dance chaperone to prevent things from getting out of control. The franco proved insufficient to fully control the unruly Dominican economy.

The US dollar took over the scene with the confidence of a sheriff restoring order to a chaotic town. The introduction of the US dollar brought stability but came with significant drawbacks. The Dominican Republic was forced to follow foreign rules. The situation felt like staying at your parents' home where you feel safe yet lack personal ownership.

The Dominican peso officially emerged in 1947 which marked a proud statement of the country's determination to remain and prosper. The Dominican peso was born like a child who reached maturity and moved away from home to forge its own path in life. The peso has experienced both successes and setbacks similar to the journey of adults through their life's challenges. Despite various challenges, the Dominican peso demonstrated resilience which reflects the Dominican people's commitment to creating a better future.

As of today the peso demonstrates national strength and represents the country's development story. The dream of stability and prosperity remains achievable despite chaos and uncertainty.

The Dominican Republic's turbulent history mirrors the peso's economic journey. The narrative depicts the relentless pursuit of economic autonomy alongside the demonstration of strength and perseverance.

Ramon was raised as a child within the oppressive regime of Trujillo's dictatorship. The sugar cane fields appear to Ramon as a vast green ocean while laborers work under overseers' scrutiny. Everywhere Ramon listens he hears tales of wealth creation but this wealth inevitably ends up in the capital enriching the luxurious homes and flashy vehicles of Trujillo's closest associates.

The small merchant Ramon's father fights hard to survive financially. The peso in his pocket diminishes daily while its value fluctuates unpredictably like the dictator's temper. A shipment of goods reaches the port but officials withhold it until they receive a bribe. After Ramon's father declines a bribe request his business faces constant inspections which delays licenses and forces him to shut down.

Trujillo's regime collapses and Ramon matures into adulthood. The post-Trujillo era brings both hope and chaos to Ramon who observes the peso's value fluctuating wildly like a ship in turbulent seas. New industries develop alongside tourism that introduces abundant foreign currency yet creates a fresh type of dependence.

Ramon launches his small business within the lively capital city. Ramon maneuvers through the intricate regulatory system while confronting ongoing corruption and the persistent influence of history. He understands the peso to represent his country's past difficulties and future goals in addition to serving as a historical reminder of lessons learned through struggle.

The digital age finds a new admirer in Ramon's young entrepreneurial son. He envisions a Dominican Republic where technology serves as an empowerment tool for all citizens and transforms the peso into an instrument for progress and inclusivity. He acknowledges the impending challenges along with global economic uncertainties and climate change threats yet he recognizes his people's resilience and their determination to construct a better future.

The peso's narrative transcends financial metrics because it embodies human aspiration and persistent hope for justice and prosperity. The Dominican Republic's currency saga persists as new generations create additional chapters in its unfolding narrative.

Under the Caribbean sun the Dominican Republic shines as a brilliant mosaic brimming with vivid colors. Merengue rhythms combined with the aroma of coffee and friendly people create a vibrant pulse throughout this island nation. Underneath the brightness of this lively façade exists a multifaceted economic narrative with the US dollar in a central role.

Think of tourism as the island's heartbeat. Year after year millions of tourists flock to the island's pristine beaches because they seek out the allure of turquoise waters and swaying palm trees. Travelers occupy resort accommodations while investigating historic sites and enjoy lively club nights. The arrival of tourists results in a massive influx of US dollars which serves as essential fuel for the nation's economic engine. A grand fiesta unfolds where everyone receives advantages starting with hotel owners and extending to street vendors who market handcrafted souvenirs.

After every good party comes the inevitable hangover of the morning after. The Dominican Republic understands that tourism cannot serve as its sole economic foundation. Constructing a home upon sand makes it vulnerable to destruction from any powerful storm. They're expanding their tourism offerings by discovering hidden waterfalls for eco-tours and promoting the vibrant culture that lies beyond the beaches. The Dominican Republic focuses on sharing its authentic spirit with visitors while making sure tourism benefits every sector of society.

The Dominican diaspora represents a widespread family network that maintains strong roots in their homeland soil while spreading throughout the world. The Dominican diaspora sends their affection and assistance through money transfers which create a continuous flow of US dollars that sustain families and enable aspirations. A lifeline exists between generations through the safety net which stands as a testament to their hard work and sacrifice.

The dependency on the US dollar functions as both a protective measure and a potential threat. When you dance with a strong partner you achieve stability at the expense of some personal freedom. The Dominican Republic is mastering the delicate task of promoting its national currency, the peso, yet recognizing the strong presence of the US dollar. The Dominican Republic moves steadily toward increased economic independence through gradual changes.

The Dominican Republic eagerly anticipates and welcomes the future ahead. The Dominican Republic strengthens its relationships with neighboring Caribbean nations by establishing a regional network dedicated to support and joint efforts. Through mobile technology it offers banking services to remote villages while riding the wave of financial innovation. The Dominican Republic plants opportunity seeds while technology and knowledge provide essential nourishment.

The real power of this narrative stems from its people. Farmers care for their plants while entrepreneurs start businesses and teachers educate future leaders. The people will determine the future path of the peso while making economic growth result in improved lives for everyone. This narrative demonstrates Dominican resilience and creativity alongside steadfast hope which stands as proof of their lasting spirit.

The Swiss Franc: A Haven of Stability in a Turbulent World

Switzerland before 1850 was not the modern nation known for precision timepieces and delectable treats but a place where currencies created chaotic confusion. Every canton functioned as an independent mint which produced its own currency leading to a vast array of over 860 distinct coin types. Merchants faced a nightmare scenario where trade became a risky gamble because of multitudinous metal coins with inconsistent values.

The Bernese thaler had different purchasing power in Zurich's marketplace compared to other locations. Every county in England possessing its own currency created a logistical nightmare. The country's fragmented financial system blocked national progress by obstructing trade and economic development.

The Old Swiss Confederacy established in 1291 functioned as a loose alliance where states maintained their independence. Every canton fiercely protected its authority to produce its own currency as a representation of its independence and self-respect. The chaotic monetary environment held back the nation from reaching its full potential.

The Helvetic Republic emerged as a French-driven effort to establish unity. During the Helvetic Republic period they established one national currency called the franc which was a silver coin modeled after the Bernese thaler. The Republic failed like a temporary illusion and the cantons returned to their previous systems.

The period of Mediation brought even greater confusion to the nation. Different currencies proliferated through the nation while foreign coins entered the economy and standardization failures slowed economic progress. Building a house out of mismatched bricks and unstable foundations accurately represents their situation.

Why was unification so difficult? Imagine herding cats! The cantons fiercely protected their independence by maintaining control over their own financial systems. Money changers benefited from the chaotic environment while they fought to protect their economic interests against changes that posed a threat. The absence of a central authority to enforce order meant cantons with varied economic systems had difficulty reaching agreement.

But change was brewing. The industrial revolution required stable currency systems which made the diverse currency system impractical due to advancements in transportation. The Swiss national identity began to take shape while a common currency became a symbol of their unity. The examples set by other European nations powered the winds of change.

The 1848 Constitution marked a critical transition by establishing a more robust federal government which acquired the authority to produce coins. The cantons had to follow the house rules just like rebellious teenagers do.

The Swiss franc came into existence when the Federal Coinage Act of 1850 established a silver-based currency that connected to the French franc. The decision was practical because it supported international trade and promoted economic development.

The transition wasn't seamless. The old cantonal coins continued to circulate after the federal currency was introduced as if they were remnants from an ancient past.

Over time the Swiss franc established its dominance which made trade operations easier and led to increased investment while promoting national cohesion.

During periods of worldwide instability the Swiss franc represented both strength and stability as a secure investment. The establishment of a unified nation in Switzerland demonstrates its evolution from an assortment of separate cantons.

The Swiss franc story illustrates how one currency united a divided land and drove economic advancement. The Swiss franc retains its symbolic power of national strength and stability as it continues to evolve through the present day.

The unchanging snow-covered mountains and untouched valleys of the Swiss Alps have stood as an emblem of Switzerland's lasting stability. The charming surface of Switzerland hides a hidden reality characterized by secure vaults and encrypted banking accounts where people generate vast wealth while maintaining confidentiality. The domain of finance in Switzerland serves as an enigmatic yet intriguing world of financial activities.

Switzerland earned its financial haven status through intentional efforts and historical decisions. The policy of neutrality Switzerland adopted centuries ago directly led to its current status. The Swiss commitment to neutrality extends beyond war avoidance because neutrality represents a core element of Swiss identity which showcases their dedication to impartiality and discretion that has made them trustworthy to many worldwide.

The Swiss banking system has achieved widespread recognition for its secrecy practices which originated in the 1930s following legal protections for Jewish clients who escaped Nazi persecution. The secrecy practiced by Swiss banks has drawn both legitimate assets and illicit funds which prompts international demands to increase transparency.

Switzerland has implemented measures to combat these issues by entering into information-sharing agreements with other nations regarding tax evaders and criminals. Switzerland maintains its pledge to client privacy while its banks uphold strong confidentiality practices.

The Swiss franc stands as a cornerstone of Switzerland's financial achievements because of its renowned stability and robust power. The Swiss franc serves as a safe haven during periods of global uncertainty because of the country's strong economy and low national debt combined with a conservative central bank.

Several elements including the privacy versus transparency debate together with emerging technologies and global investor requirements will influence Switzerland's financial future. However, one thing is certain: The financial success of Switzerland will remain firmly rooted in its dedication to stability alongside its neutrality and discretion.

The Swiss franc has maintained its exceptional stability throughout the global financial turmoil while demonstrating strong resilience during the globalization era. The Swiss franc maintained stability during the interconnected era through challenges and changes that demonstrated Switzerland's dedication to sound economic practices.

The world's financial systems have become tightly interwoven through globalization which results in money crossing borders almost instantaneously. Global financial changes have dramatically influenced currencies such as the Swiss franc which investors regard as a secure asset during global market turbulence.

When global crises occur investor demand for the franc increases and its value rises which leads to more expensive Swiss exports and could damage the Swiss economy. The Swiss National Bank must balance the franc's value through careful management to prevent it from becoming either excessively strong or weak.

The 2008 financial crisis marked a pivotal turning point in the history of the franc. During the financial system's near collapse worldwide investors turned to the franc for safety which resulted in its value climbing high. The SNB took decisive action by purchasing other currencies to prevent the franc from becoming too strong while defending the Swiss economy.

The Eurozone crisis introduced additional complexity to the financial landscape. Concerns about the euro's stability led investors to view the franc as a secure option. In an unprecedented action that demonstrated its dedication to stability the SNB established a minimum exchange rate with the euro.

Switzerland has carried out a careful balancing act to address these challenges. The SNB has implemented multiple tools such as currency interventions along with interest rate adjustments and clear communication methods to maintain stability. The franc's appeal has grown because of the country's robust economy together with low debt levels and a skilled workforce alongside its reputation for innovation.

Looking ahead, the franc faces new questions. The SNB's bold strategy to implement negative interest rates with the goal of weakening the franc has produced inconsistent outcomes. The development of digital currencies such as Bitcoin and potential CBDCs creates opportunities while bringing new challenges.

The franc maintains its enduring appeal because of its stable nature despite prevailing uncertainties. The franc stands as a reliable store of value because it relies on a robust economy and dependable central bank management during unpredictable times.

Although the future financial landscape remains unpredictable the Swiss franc stands ready to adjust. The Swiss franc displays resilience thanks to Switzerland's legacy of innovation together with its openness to novel concepts and dedication to stability. The SNB must maintain their vigilance and flexibility while communicating clearly to successfully tackle upcoming challenges.

The Swiss franc's evolution throughout the globalized world demonstrates its lasting power. The narrative of the Swiss franc demonstrates ongoing adjustments to new challenges which will extend into the future. The stability of the franc provides confidence to both Switzerland and the entire global financial system.

The Canadian Dollar: Navigating the Currents of a North American Economy

The early Canadian money system functioned as a chaotic marketplace of diverse currencies. The lively market buzzed with trade talk and the sound of coins as diverse Spanish doubloons, French francs, Portuguese escudos and British shillings filled your view instead of typical currency forms. In colonial Canada my friend you'd find a monetary system that matched the diversity of its people.

Now, picture this: In 18th-century Halifax you operate as a merchant while figuring out how to navigate the complex world of diverse currencies. You have a Spanish dollar with several French coins and even some government-issued playing cards. The government decided to release playing cards as currency during a period of desperation. What method do you use to assess their monetary worth? The "Halifax Rating" system emerged as a method to establish local currency values for foreign coins to bring structure to monetary disorder. The Halifax Rating system functioned as an early form of currency exchange system which lacked precision and exhibited regional differences.

What led to the creation of such an eclectic currency assortment? Visualize youthful Canada as it maintained its colonial dependence while struggling to obtain legitimate British money. The colonists developed creative solutions to their financial limitations because scarcity encouraged innovation and they adopted a practical approach of using whatever resources were available. As a symbol of early American influence the Spanish dollar gained widespread trust and became the economic backbone of daily transactions. The Spanish dollar proved so dependable that it surpassed the official British pound sterling in effectiveness.

The pound served as the standard benchmark which acted as a spectral presence above the colonies. While financial records used pounds, shillings, and pence as their standard units of measurement the tangible coins themselves were nearly nonexistent. The British Empire's mercantilist strategies aimed to accumulate precious metals within its territories caused this situation. Britain maintained an approach where colonies should manage their finances in British currency but wouldn't supply the necessary coins.

The growth in commerce between the American colonies and other regions strengthened their currency's power. The Spanish dollar followed by the US dollar gained popularity which led to monetary competition reflecting the political tensions of their era. The battle for monetary dominance between the old world powers and the emerging new world forced the colonies into a precarious financial position.

And then there were the playing cards. Yes, you heard that right! Faced with depleted treasury reserves the colonial government of New France began to issue signed playing cards as IOUs. It's a scene ripe for historical fiction: A soldier exhausted from his duties receives payment through a deck of playing cards with hopes of exchanging them for actual currency before the next card game begins.

Local merchants' tokens became a new player during this period of monetary chaos. Comparable to modern loyalty cards these tokens functioned solely at their respective merchant stores. Merchants implemented an ingenious system to maintain commerce while encouraging repeat customers during economic hardship.

The emergence of numerous banks throughout the early 1800s led to the introduction of banknotes issued by these institutions. The introduction of banknotes from different banks created an additional level to the currency structure since the value of each bank's currency was proportional to its reputation. During this period colonies experienced advancements together with doubt while they faced difficulties of a rapidly developing financial system.

The demand for a single national currency became increasingly prominent by mid-century. The mixture of coins, banknotes, and tokens created an unsustainable financial system for an expanding nation. The Canadian dollar was created in 1858 through a compromise that integrated elements from both British and American monetary systems. The Canadian dollar maintained stability through its peg to the US dollar while remaining compatible with the British gold sovereign to achieve a diplomatic financial equilibrium between North America and Europe.

Canada's adoption of its own dollar marked a critical turning point that showcased the nation's development toward economic independence and maturity. The establishment of a stable currency brought structure to disorder and enabled future prosperity. The Canadian economy demonstrated its capacity to integrate traditional practices with modern developments while managing its complex ties to both Britain and the United States.

When you hold a Canadian dollar in your hand think about its vibrant history which started with a chaotic assortment of foreign coins alongside playing cards and local merchants' tokens. The narrative highlights human adaptability and innovative strength as people persevere during periods of financial chaos.

Ah, the Loonie and the Greenback! This complex relationship between the Loonie and the Greenback has evolved into a full-scale family drama that unfolds before a global audience. Imagine this:

The Loonie, which embodies a free-spirited nature, demonstrates a deep connection to the natural world. Imagine a sturdy woodsman who has pure intentions but loves adventure while secretly desiring the security of his warm cabin. He possesses an extraordinary ability to discover valuable resources beneath the Earth such as oil, lumber and minerals and experiences mood fluctuations according to the market value of his findings. Soaring oil prices make him walk with regal confidence. He withdraws to his cabin to reflect on life while enjoying maple syrup whenever prices drop.

His older brother named Greenback serves as a banker on Wall Street. His sense of responsibility is evident through his constant business attire and the briefcase he carries. People always seek his attention because he captivates everyone wherever he goes. His ego might seem prominent but it is supported by his substantial experience and authority. He understands that everyone revolves around him because he is the center of attention.

These two brothers remain inseparable even though they have many differences between them. The brothers have homes next to each other which border the world's most extensive unguarded backyard. The neighbors regularly come over to host barbecues while sharing tools and exchanging favors. Their lives remain connected through every good and bad circumstance.

Picture their parents as The Bank of Canada serving as mom and the Federal Reserve acting as dad. Mom works tirelessly to maintain harmony by ensuring Loonie doesn't lose control while Greenback refrains from bullying behaviors. She desires success for both her sons yet understands they must experience their own life lessons. While the mom stays actively involved in their affairs the dad maintains a more relaxed approach. His responsibilities extend beyond these two because he has the entire world to manage. He maintains strict vigilance over the situation and stands ready to step forward if chaos emerges.

The peculiar behavior of their family generates endless discussion among their neighbors (the global economy). When the brothers maintain peace it brings comfort to everyone. Whenever they have a disagreement the entire neighborhood experiences the tension.

The family therapist functions like the currency exchange rate. His role involves listening to their complaints while observing their interactions and making sense of the situation. He converts their emotional states and fears into a universally intelligible language.

How are current conditions affecting the relationship between the Loonie and Greenback? We are in 2025 right now but the atmosphere feels tense. The state of the world creates confusion and widespread anxiety among people. Greenback feels stressed about inflation combined with global conflicts which leads him to increase interest rates thereby making borrowing more costly for all parties including Loonie. Loonie remains composed as the volatile oil prices cause his stress levels to spike. The Bank of Canada (referred to as Mom) strives for stability while navigating a precarious situation. While she has to pay attention to Dad's (the Fed's) actions she must also protect Loonie's interests.

Will they make it through? Of course they will. They always do. Their relationship might involve fights and frustrations but they remain family at their core. Family members remain united and supportive through difficult times.

This narrative explores the complex relationship between the Loonie and the Greenback who share a brotherly bond and experience shifting relational dynamics. This narrative keeps developing while showcasing dramatic events and the persistent strength of family connections.

Subtopic 3: The Bank of Canada stands as Canada's economic captain beyond its physical structure.

Ottawa's old bank building doesn't reflect the true essence of this institution. The Bank of Canada functions as the captain of Canada's economic vessel while navigating through the turbulent seas of the international financial system. Their mission? The Bank of Canada works to ensure stable economic conditions while steering clear of recessionary icebergs and inflationary storms.

The Loonie's Guardian Angel:

How does our national currency, the "loonie," perform its role on the global financial stage? The Bank of Canada serves as a protective guardian angel for the currency. The Bank of Canada doesn't manage every action of the Canadian dollar but possesses strong instruments for guidance like the interest rate adjustments. When interest rates rise the loonie tends to take flight whereas lower interest rates cause it to lose altitude. Maintaining the

Canadian economy's health depends entirely on achieving the ideal balance.

Battling the Inflation Dragon:

Inflation operates as a stealthy monster that devours your well-earned money through its fiery breath. The Bank of Canada's ultimate tool to fight economic challenges remains its "policy interest rate." The policy interest rate functions as the primary control mechanism that influences all other interest rates throughout the economy. The Bank increases its policy interest rate when inflation emerges as a problem which results in higher borrowing costs. The policy interest rate acts as a cooling mechanism for spending which helps to subdue the inflation dragon by reducing the heat under a boiling pot.

The Bank aims to maintain inflation at a steady rate of 2%. The "sweet spot" maintains predictable pricing which helps everyone organize their financial plans effectively.

Nurturing Growth, the Gentle Way:

The Bank of Canada seeks both to manage inflation and to ensure the Canadian economy develops and expands. The Bank of Canada rejects any rapid growth patterns which prove to be short-lived. Their goal is to achieve sustainable growth which develops progressively like a healthy plant flourishing over time. By reducing interest rates policymakers encourage borrowing and spending thereby providing a subtle economic boost.

Crisis Mode: Navigating Global Storms:

Global financial systems are linked together with the potential for sudden economic crises that impact nations worldwide. The Bank of Canada needs to maintain readiness to intervene during financial storms. Did you recall the 2008 financial meltdown or the COVID-19 pandemic? The Bank responded rapidly by cutting interest rates and purchasing government bonds which allowed them to pump essential cash into the financial system. The central bank acts as a life preserver to support the economy through unstable periods.

New Challenges on the Horizon:

Fast forward to 2025. Supply chains remain entangled while energy prices continue to fluctuate alongside the ongoing global economic recovery. The Bank of Canada faces tough decisions. Quick interest rate increases might damage economic recovery while delayed adjustments to interest rates could trigger high inflation. Canadian economic stability requires constant monitoring of international dynamics such as geopolitical conflicts and unexpected oil price changes that impact the nation.

The Bank is adopting innovative tools and strategies to overcome current challenges. The public now receives clear explanations from the Bank as they share their decision-making processes more openly. Canadians remain informed and confident about the Bank's direction because of transparency and trust.

Subtopic 4: The Digital Loonie and Beyond: A Brave New World of Money

Prepare for a fast-paced revolution in financial systems as the world of money undergoes rapid transformation. Digital payment methods have replaced cash as the predominant form of transaction. The Bank of Canada leads the charge by examining and exploring the potential of digital financial systems.

The Digital Loonie: A Digital Cousin to Your Wallet

The Bank of Canada has developed an idea for a digital version of the Canadian dollar. The idea of a central bank digital currency (CBDC) has been given the name "digital loonie." The digital loonie functions differently from Bitcoin because it acts as a digital version of your physical cash.

The Bank of Canada is conducting thorough research on digital currency possibilities while assessing both benefits and drawbacks before making a decision.

Why Go Digital?

A digital loonie could offer several advantages:

Faster, Cheaper Payments: You could send money between countries at incredible speed while paying only small transaction fees.
Financial Inclusion for All: A digital loonie would enable people who lack bank accounts to participate in the digital economy.
Sparking Innovation: The digital loonie would motivate businesses to develop more innovative payment solutions.
Staying in Control: A digital loonie would provide the Bank of Canada with necessary control to preserve its monetary policy authority amid the growth of private cryptocurrencies.

Navigating the Challenges:

The digital world presents multiple challenges that complicate its operation. There are some serious challenges to consider:

Protecting Privacy: What strategies can be implemented to maintain user privacy while preventing criminal activities in digital currency networks?
Ensuring Security: Since a digital loonie would likely become a major target for cyber attackers robust security measures become essential.
Maintaining Financial Stability: Moving to a digital loonie requires a careful approach because such a change could destabilize the banking system.
Bridging the Digital Divide: Access to technology and necessary skills is not universal which makes accessibility for everyone an essential requirement.

Financial Inclusion: Leaving No One Behind

The Bank of Canada works to include all individuals in financial services by making essential financial services available to everyone regardless of their background or location. A digital loonie has potential benefits but cannot serve as a stand-alone solution. Successful implementation requires simultaneous efforts to expand internet access and improve digital literacy together with better access to devices.

The Future of Money: A Dynamic Landscape

New technologies such as stablecoins and decentralized finance (DeFi) alongside fintech companies continue to transform the global money landscape. The Bank of Canada remains vigilant about evolving financial trends while adapting their strategies to preserve Canada's position as a global financial leader.

Hypothetical 2025: A Glimpse into the Future

Imagine it's 2025. The Bank of Canada started a pilot project to test digital loonies in select communities while collecting valuable feedback as private digital currencies continue to gain popularity. Global central banks have joined forces with the Bank of Canada to share expertise and establish collaborative strategies that lead to a secure and functional worldwide financial system which includes everyone.

The discussion focus now moves from technological aspects toward human impact which guarantees universal advantages from digital advancements. The Bank of Canada works to create a prosperous financial future for every Canadian citizen.

The Bank of Canada: Your Partner in Financial Well-being

The Bank of Canada functions as a referee that maintains both fairness and stability within the financial system. They dedicate themselves relentlessly to simplify how people understand and navigate finance. The Bank leads the digital future while Canadians continue to support them. Digital loonies will soon arrive to create a financial system that is both efficient and accessible for everyone. The Bank of Canada has prepared for future developments so Canadians can follow their lead.

Remember: The text you provided can be understood in multiple ways and this represents one possible interpretation. The objective involves increasing engagement and relatability while maintaining essential information. The template allows you to personalize it according to your unique audience needs and communication goals.

The Japanese Yen: A Currency of Transformation, Innovation, and Resilience

In pre-1868 Japan markets were full of life and each market operated with its distinct currency system. It's a scene straight out of an Edo period drama: In busy marketplaces, merchants conducted price negotiations while they precisely measured gold and silver and measured rice stacks. Pre-Meiji Japan existed as a country filled with different forms of money rather than serving as a mere setting for historical films.

Every province or han in Japan functioned as a distinct piece of a complex economic jigsaw puzzle. Ancient Chinese coins which had become smooth from prolonged use circulated together with new Japanese copies. To demonstrate their power feudal lords introduced their unique paper currency known as hansatsu which only possessed value inside their territory. The traditional system remained entrenched in complex operations.

Regional trading routes demanded the skills of a labyrinth navigator. Business travelers from Osaka to Edo required expertise in exchange rates and calculation skills alongside negotiation abilities. The presence of counterfeit coins alongside unstable values continually threatened economic stability while the absence of a cohesive system restricted national growth thus maintaining the feudal fragmentation of the nation.

The Meiji Restoration erupted like a thunderclap that shattered the old foundations of Japan. The emperor transitioned from being a mere symbolic leader to becoming a central figure as the nation began its rapid journey toward modernization. The new government looked to Western models to shape a Japan that could assert itself internationally.

The old currency system presented a major obstacle that needed to be overcome to reach modernization goals. Japan created a modern currency called the yen when they introduced it in 1871. The yen demonstrated unity and progress through its decimal system and standardized coins. The currency reform eradicated outdated problems which opened the nation to dynamic economic growth.

After its establishment in 1882 the Bank of Japan took on the role of managing the new monetary system by overseeing the yen and maintaining economic stability. State-of-the-art machinery at the Osaka Mint produced shining coins which demonstrated Japan's industrial excellence.

The yen's impact was transformative. Commerce expanded between domestic regions of Japan and reached out to international markets. International capital inflows supported industrial expansion and drove Japan toward modernization. The yen emerged as a mark of national pride that illustrated Japan's transformation from feudal seclusion into a powerhouse of the global economy.

Throughout its journey Japan faced numerous obstacles. The value of yen experienced volatility alongside rising inflation and global events impacted Japan's economic stability. The yen demonstrated its strong resilience repeatedly despite various economic challenges.

The yen maintains its position among the top global currencies which reflects the successful vision of the Meiji reformers. Japan investigates digital currency advancements while the yen adapts to meet the requirements of a fast-paced evolving world.

Japan's national narrative is mirrored in the yen which demonstrates the country's ambition and innovative spirit alongside its persistent strength. The currency of a nation represents its unique identity and the values it holds while also reflecting its future aspirations.

The yen emerged from World War II like a phoenix rising from its ashes. As it flew through the skies the yen raised Japan to unparalleled economic prosperity. The yen endured fiery trials and stages of decline before it could rise again.

Japanese products became irresistible worldwide because the yen acted as a magical economic force in the post-war period. Toyota along with Sony and Panasonic emerged as household names which served as symbols for quality products that were affordable. The yen's fixed rate of 360 to the dollar acted as Japan's economic miracle's secret ingredient.

But the world was changing. The collapse of the Bretton Woods system resulted in the yen gaining full independence. The yen started soaring upward much like a kite caught in powerful wind currents. This posed a new challenge. Japanese enterprises needed to boost their innovation levels and streamline their processes to maintain competitive superiority.

The Plaza Accord brought together major economic powers to control the strong yen. Holding back the tidal wave proved impossible. Japan's economy experienced a speculative frenzy when the yen surged in value. When the bubble burst Japan entered a period of ten years of economic stagnation.

But the yen's story didn't end there. Abenomics represented a daring economic trial which aimed to rekindle economic growth. Japan utilized the yen as a strategic instrument to fight against deflation. The central bank introduced a monetary stimulus to the economy with the intention of depreciating the yen value to strengthen Japanese export performance.

Japan's transformation throughout history is mirrored in the evolution of the yen. Japan moved from devastation to economic strength by continuously evolving and finding new paths. The yen has transformed from a mere export currency into an advanced international currency that operates within a complicated economic environment.

Looking ahead, the yen faces new uncertainties. The US dollar remains a formidable rival. China's economic ascent brings significant changes to the world stage. The demographic problems within Japan extend their influence far into the future.

The yen exhibits the same remarkable resilience that characterizes Japan's national character. It has weathered storms and emerged stronger. Japan's capacity to innovate alongside its ability to adapt and secure its position in the rapidly evolving global environment will determine the future of the yen.

Beyond its function as currency the yen represents Japan's enduring economic strength. The yen represents Japan's economic power together with its persistent strength and lasting spirit. The narrative of this story remains ongoing as it weaves through many unexpected turns alongside its persistent trials and victories.

The once unbeatable Japan resembles a noble samurai now struggling with the physical decline of old age as well as the visible wounds from its historical conflicts. This narrative reveals the mighty warrior's stumble and its continuous journey towards regaining its former strength.

The Plaza Accord: A Sudden Shift in the Tide

Visualize an epic sumo wrestling battle occurring in the year 1985. America stood tall with its strong dollar showing its power on one side. Japan stood strong against its competitors as its currency started to appreciate. The Plaza Accord acted as a referee intervening to push the dollar lower while lifting the value of the yen. The agreement aimed to benefit America but disrupted Japan's export-focused economic system.

The Yen's Rise: A Blessing and a Curse

The yen surged upward as swiftly as wind caught the samurai's sails pushing it ahead yet making control increasingly difficult. Japan's export-driven strength faced challenges as exports became pricier. The Bank of Japan acted as a prudent elder when it tackled the situation by reducing interest rates to smooth the transition. The government removed constraints from the samurai's armor to increase its flexibility.

The Bubble: A Fleeting Illusion of Wealth

The low interest rates produced an unforeseen consequence. A powerful sense of perpetual prosperity intoxicated the nation similar to a potent sake. Both individuals and businesses succumbed to the excitement and borrowed excessively to place investments in stock markets and real estate without regard for the future. The value of land reached unprecedented levels, turning the earth beneath people's feet into gold.

The Crash: A Rude Awakening

But like all bubbles, this one burst. The Bank of Japan identified the threat and increased interest rates which acted like a shock of cold water awakening intoxicated party-goers. A stock market crash combined with a real estate price collapse devastated numerous people. The samurai who had become intoxicated with triumph suddenly lost their balance and collapsed.

The Lost Decades: A Long and Winding Road

Japan experienced a prolonged and severe winter of economic challenges following the burst of its economic bubble. The land experienced a chilling deflationary wind which discouraged people from spending money and making investments. Businesses withered, and unemployment rose. The dynamic economy stopped growing as if a samurai warrior had been caught in a timeless moment.

Abenomics: A Bold Attempt at Revival

Shinzo Abe became Japan's charismatic leader in 2012 as he developed a revitalization plan for the nation. His three-pronged plan called Abenomics acted as acupuncture needles targeting essential economic areas to boost their activity. A powerful money wave burst from the Bank of Japan designed to rescue the economy from its stagnant state. The government expanded its investment efforts as if a blacksmith was crafting new instruments to drive economic growth. Structural reforms functioned as a rigorous training program to create a more adaptive and competitive economy.

The Digital Yen: A Glimpse into the Future

Japan is currently researching the digital yen which acts like a futuristic katana that could outperform traditional currency with greater precision and flexibility. The digital yen promises to transform payment systems while providing financial access to those without bank accounts and enabling the central bank to acquire additional economic regulatory tools. The introduction of the digital yen brings about worries related to privacy protection as well as financial system security and stability.

The Future: A Balancing Act

Japan's future is like a tightrope walk. Japan faces the challenge of managing both its aging population along with overwhelming national debt. The potential of technology as well as tourism alongside a more inclusive workforce offers a positive counterpoint. Despite being wounded the samurai maintains enough wisdom and resilience along with innovative thinking to find his way across this hazardous path.

The world remains on edge as Japan, now an elder warrior nation, embarks on a path of transformation. The world waits to see if Japan will restore its lost grandeur or fall victim to global transformations. Only time will tell. But one thing is certain: The story of Japan represents the relentless human spirit through its adaptive capabilities and innovative efforts toward a brighter future.

The Swedish Krona: A Currency of Social Democracy and Global Competitiveness

Ah, Scandinavia! The land famous for Vikings and fjords embraces a unified currency system. You bet! Our time machine transports us back to the 19th century where Sweden, Denmark, and Norway came together to establish a shared monetary system.

Picture this: It's 1873. Transport yourself to 1873 and visualize those sophisticated gentlemen with top hats negotiating business while enjoying a glass of aquavit (no surprise that it's a Scandinavian schnapps!). Why not establish a shared currency among us? they slurred, "Think of the trade deals!" And boom! The Scandinavian Monetary Union was born.

The Scandinavian Monetary Union acted as a financial embrace uniting these Nordic countries together. Sweden and Denmark initiated the collaboration and Norway became part of the agreement two years afterward. They ditched their old currencies and introduced a shiny new one, pegged to gold: The new currency that united Sweden, Denmark, and Norway was known as the krona (or krone depending on who you ask). This currency system represented the euro equivalent of its era yet featured strikingly fashionable headwear.

Why bother with all this? Just picture yourself attempting to purchase a scrumptious Danish pastry using Swedish riksdaler as payment. Confusing, right? The Union made trading simpler for these nations to exchange herring, timber and adorable little wooden horses. Plus, everyone loved the stability of gold. The gold standard held the same universal trust that Beyoncé commands in the entertainment industry.

For a while, things were awesome. Economic stability emerged as booming trade fostered a sense of communal financial unity among nations. The outbreak of World War I disrupted the economic stability of the time. World War I disrupted global order and destroyed the gold standard system. The economic order appeared to have been disrupted by an unseen hand who threw economic turmoil into the mix.

The Union faded away gradually until it disappeared just like a New Year's resolution people forget. By the 1920s people resumed their independent ways while the legacy endured. The krona/krone names stuck around as a sweet memory of their past monetary partnership.

And guess what? The Nordic countries are still besties! Even though they no longer share a single currency system with each other the Nordic countries continue to work together across many areas as if they were a group of kids who really get along.

Now, fast forward to 2025. Sweden has mastered managing the krona to maintain its value across the global economic landscape. Denmark maintains its currency while watching the euro developments with an open mind about future possibilities and Norway? Norway maintains its independence while keeping its currency strong and separate.

So, what's the moral of the story? Money matters show that sharing remains a caring act. The Scandinavian Monetary Union exists only in history books yet it serves as evidence that teamwork between nations can create prosperous periods which eventually fade away. And hey, who knows? A new Nordic super-currency could emerge someday. Just imagine the possibilities... and the hats!

The Swedish Model: A Balancing Act on the High Wire

A society where all citizens receive healthcare and education exists as a fundamental right while unemployment remains a non-issue. Sounds like a utopia, right? Well, Sweden comes pretty close. Sweden maintains its "Swedish Model" by masterfully balancing a strong welfare system with an intensely competitive market economy. The Krona serves as Sweden's balancing pole in their tightrope walk through their unique economic model.

What is this Swedish Model?

Envision this model as a multi-ingredient recipe.

Social Security: A fail-safe social security system ensures that nobody slips through because it's woven so tightly. Healthcare, education, unemployment benefits—all readily available.
Equality: The model levels the playing field so that everyone can pursue success without discrimination based on their background.
Economic Growth: The Swedish Model requires businesses to maintain their competitive edge globally while fostering an environment of innovation and prosperity.
Labor Harmony: The collaboration between unions and employers operates smoothly like a well-oiled machine.

The Krona: A Free Spirit

The Krona operates independently compared to currencies tied to others like the Euro. The Krona experiences fluctuations as its value goes up or down with the trends of the international market. Sweden has the capability to guide its economy through interest rate adjustments to control inflation and manage economic growth.

The Krona's Impact: A Ripple Effect

Exports: As the Krona weakens it reduces the international prices of Swedish goods which increases exports and improves economic performance.
Imports: The devalued currency results in higher prices for imported products which imposes financial strain on consumers.
Inflation: Swedish central bank Riksbank monitors the Krona to control inflation with precision comparable to a skilled archer hitting the bullseye.

The Swedish Model's Successes: A Shining Beacon

High Standard of Living: Swedes benefit from a highly enviable standard of living which includes exceptional healthcare services and education systems along with robust social welfare support.
Low Inequality: The wealth disparity in Sweden is significantly less than that of many countries which leads to a more balanced social structure.
Innovation: Innovation thrives throughout Sweden as it continuously expands the limits of technology and knowledge.
Strong Economy: The Swedish economy stands strong despite high taxation levels because it demonstrates how economic competitiveness and social responsibility can exist together.

This section examines how countries face difficulties while operating in an integrated global environment.

Despite its strengths Sweden confronts multiple challenges amid today's globally connected environment.

Low-Wage Competition: Businesses may move their production operations to low-wage countries which creates downward pressure on wage levels in Sweden.
Welfare State Sustainability: The welfare state receives funding from high taxes which simultaneously act as a deterrent for businesses. It's a constant balancing act.
Technological Disruption: The job market landscape undergoes transformation through AI and automation as workers need to acquire new skills for adaptation.
Global Economic Shocks: Sweden's open economic system resembles a ship facing a storm which exposes its vulnerability to worldwide events such as economic downturns and pandemics.
Demographic Shifts: The welfare system faces increased burdens because the number of retirees grows while the workforce diminishes.
Brain Drain: The continuous struggle to prevent skilled individuals from pursuing better opportunities overseas remains a significant issue.
Currency Volatility: Businesses face uncertainty due to the unpredictable value of the Krona.
External Shocks: International developments outside Sweden's reach have the potential to destabilize the Krona's value.

Sweden's Response: Charting a Course

Sweden isn't sitting idly by. They're tackling these challenges head-on:

Investing in Education: Preparing employees with future job-specific skills.
Promoting Innovation: Fostering a culture of creativity and invention.

Active Labor Market Policies: Sweden puts efforts into both aiding jobless individuals to secure employment and bolstering business operations.
Fiscal Responsibility: Keeping the nation's finances in order.
International Cooperation: International Cooperation requires collaboration with foreign nations to solve worldwide problems.
Pension Reform: The pension system requires modification to match demographic changes.
Union Negotiations: Union Negotiations focus on maintaining equilibrium between employee protections and economic competitiveness.

The Euro Debate: To Join or Not to Join?

Despite being a member of the European Union Sweden continues to use its own currency instead of the Euro. This debate generates intense debate because both sides present compelling arguments.

Pro-Euro: Reduced transaction costs, increased price stability.
Anti-Euro: Loss of monetary control, reduced flexibility.

The Future: Uncharted Waters

While the Swedish Model will continue to develop over time its essential principles of social security, equality, and economic growth will remain intact.

The Krona will stay an important economic asset due to its flexibility which presents various challenges.

Sweden must keep adjusting to remain competitive while maintaining its social protection system. Maintaining equilibrium demands continuous attention and innovative strategies.

Key Issues to Watch:

Digitalization: Sweden must find ways to manage the digital revolution which will affect both its employment sector and the stability of the Krona.
Sustainability: Does Sweden have the capability to sustain its green growth leadership and remain competitive?
Global Trade: What strategies will Sweden implement in response to changing global trade patterns?
Geopolitical Risks: What steps will Sweden take to protect its economy and the Krona from global instability?

Conclusion: A Unique Path

The Swedish nation has created its own distinct path by integrating social welfare programs with market economy principles. Within this fragile ecosystem the Krona has proven to be essential.

Despite its imperfections the Swedish Model stands out as a success story for delivering a high standard of living alongside equality and innovation. The Swedish Model serves as an exemplary paradigm that merits observation and adoption.

Subtopic 3: Sweden's relationship with the euro ended before they could become a couple.

Sweden and the euro? Sweden and the euro relationship resembles that couple everyone assumed would get married but ended up breaking up. Sweden belongs to the EU but they decided not to adopt the euro. Sweden maintains its unique currency called the krona which their citizens value highly.

Sweden held a referendum regarding joining the eurozone back in 2003. The referendum was as suspenseful as the climax of a reality TV show. The majority of voters rejected eurozone membership which resulted in the euro remaining unadopted by Sweden. Why the cold feet? Well, Swedes had some serious concerns.

Picture being in a partnership where someone else holds the financial reins. Not ideal, right? The way Swedes felt about the European Central Bank (ECB) deciding their interest rates was comparable to feeling like someone else controlled their finances. The Swedes feared that their economy would be overshadowed by the broader European Central Bank's strategies.

Think of it this way: While Sweden struggles with economic issues the eurozone celebrates a financial boom. The European Central Bank may ignore Sweden's economic symptoms which could actually exacerbate their situation. The krona gives Sweden the power to independently select appropriate treatments for its economic challenges.

But it wasn't just about the economy. The krona represents a cherished family treasure that stands for Sweden's historical independence. The decision to abandon it felt as if they were sacrificing a cherished part of their identity.

Those who supported "yes" presented several legitimate arguments. Adopting the euro would enhance trade relationships while simplifying operations for businesses and amplifying Sweden's influence within Europe. Ultimately the appeal of sovereignty along with the fear of losing command outweighed all other considerations.

Sweden maintains its independent course in global economic affairs and pursues its own path. Will they ever reconcile with the euro? Only time will tell. Sweden currently appears to be happy with their unique economic relationship with their own currency.

Subtopic 4: Sweden Advances into Digital Currency with the E-Krona

Sweden leads the way like a friend who never falls behind trends. As the majority of people continue to struggle with cash payments Sweden operates almost completely without physical money. Payment cards and mobile transactions dominate Sweden's financial scene while they explore developing a central bank digital currency known as the e-krona.

Visualize electronic money that benefits from central bank security and support. Unlike unpredictable cryptocurrencies this digital krona has government approval and offers secure vault-like protection.

Why is Sweden considering this digital leap? They want to guarantee public access to central bank money continues even after physical cash ceases to exist. The initiative represents a communal resource in a city dominated by exclusive private spaces.

But it's not just about access. The e-krona represents a transformative tool that ensures payments become both quicker and more cost-effective while boosting efficiency. The e-krona represents a technological leap similar to moving from a horse-drawn carriage to a modern Tesla.

Sweden's environmental consciousness is essential to its identity which ensures they evaluate how the e-krona will impact the planet. Efforts are underway to make the e-krona environmentally friendly, akin to a solar-powered Tesla.

This digital journey encounters its own unique difficulties. What methods exist to safeguard personal data within our digital environment? What measures can be implemented to defend the system against hackers aiming to steal digital krona? The Riksbank faces these challenging questions.

The e-krona remains in pilot testing which functions much like a car test drive before final purchase. The Riksbank works on improvements while testing the system and collecting input from future users.

The introduction of the e-krona will not eliminate the need for physical cash in circulation. The e-krona and cash should function as a dynamic duo to combat financial crime and inefficiency.

The Swedish approach to implementing the e-krona demonstrates careful consideration and deliberate planning. They prefer a methodical approach and ensure that every step is carefully executed before advancing. Just as you shouldn't remove a cake from the oven until it reaches full preparation stage.

The e-krona is only one part of Sweden's broader role as a center for financial technological breakthroughs. Fintech firms emerge rapidly across the financial landscape creating innovative payment solutions and services. It's like a Silicon Valley for finance.

Sweden monitors the global economy while addressing the difficulties presented by globalization and digital advances together with environmental change. They maintain long-term stability by tailoring their policies for sustainable financial growth.

Sweden combines time-tested methods with modern advancements to create its monetary policy framework. While they cherish their autonomy they welcome innovative concepts similar to how a knowledgeable owl would operate a smartphone. Their sustainability commitment reflects a PhD economist who embraces environmental causes. They prioritize maintaining a stable and efficient financial system similar to how a master chess player plans their next move.

The Danish Krone: Stability and Pragmatism in the Heart of Europe

Ah, Denmark! The land of Vikings, hygge, and... money? You bet! The story of Danish currency begins with resonant silver pennies from the past and evolves into today's modern kroner which rustles in wallets.

From Pennies to Marks: A Viking's Wallet

Envision a powerful Viking warrior producing the first Danish currency with a handful of silver pennies. The coins you hold in your hand should not be mistaken for those splendidly engraved kroner. These practical coins were rough little discs that usually resembled their English counterparts. The value of silver coins depended on their weight rather than any royal insignia.

But wait, there's more! The "mark" served as a unit of account which functioned like the Excel spreadsheet of its era. Do you need to calculate the total amount taken from a raid? Mark it down! The shared financial system across Scandinavia demonstrates that Vikings had to manage their finances just like everyone else.

Silver Shenanigans: When Coins Got Clipped

Picture a medieval ruler who used his cunning to manipulate the purity of silver coins. Debasing the coinage, they called it. The coins were extended by adding lower-cost metals throughout their production. But people weren't fooled! Imagine the distrust: "Is this penny actually worth a penny?"

The practice of secretly clipping coins emerged as a stealthy art form. The crafty process of coin debasement involved carefully trimming small amounts of silver from coins in several places. This practice appeared trivial at first glance but accumulated substantial amounts similar to a medieval form of skimming.

Monetary Unions: A Nordic Tango

Have you ever shared a bank account with your brothers or sisters? The drama of early Scandinavian monetary unions reaches epic proportions when you expand sibling bank account sharing into a thousandfold scale. The Kalmar Union connected Denmark Sweden and Norway as they tested the viability of a unified currency.

Ambitious? Absolutely. Successful? Not so much. Political disputes and economic competition continually obstructed their progress. This story is like the old saying "too many cooks in the kitchen" but uses crowns instead of spoons.

The Rigsdaler: A Royal Rollercoaster

By the 17th century the rigsdaler emerged as the primary currency. This development represented significant progress towards the establishment of the modern krone that people appreciate today. The rigsdaler's value experienced extreme fluctuations throughout its history. The rigsdaler experienced extreme fluctuations because of wars and economic difficulties alongside inconsistent government policies.

We should also remember when paper money made its debut! You no longer needed to haul coin-filled sacks since a simple piece of paper now promised wealth. Convenient? Yes. Risky? Definitely. The economy faces inflation threats when promises become excessive.

The Krone is Born: A Golden Age

The mid-1800s signaled Denmark's readiness to transform its currency system. International trade reached new heights while the old rigsdaler system appeared as archaic as a powdered wig. Enter the krone, gleaming with gold-standard credibility!

This wasn't just a Danish affair. The Scandinavian Monetary Union resumed with Sweden and Norway adopting the krone currency. The Scandinavian Monetary Union demonstrated Nordic harmony through trade and cooperation until World War I disrupted their successful partnership.

Humans of the Krone: Tales of Change

The marketplace would have been buzzing when people exchanged the first crisp kroner for goods and services. Shopkeepers hurriedly adjusted their prices while bankers worked frantically to exchange old coins and regular people tried to understand the new currency system.

Some individuals gained while others lost as rumors spread about newfound wealth and devastating losses. The krone represented not only numerical value but also human lives and economic activities in daily commerce.

The Krone Today: Digital Dreams and National Pride

The Danish krone stands as a symbol of effective financial governance and characteristic Scandinavian determination to remain independent from the Euro currency. The krone remains susceptible to global economic transformations.

Digital payments through tap-and-go transactions are overtaking cash as the preferred method of payment. Who knows? Perhaps the krone will eventually become nothing more than a digital memory of its former physical presence through clinking coins and rustling banknotes.

But one thing's for sure: The historical evolution of Denmark's money system demonstrates a narrative of resilience and adaptation reflecting how national identity has been integrated into its currency from Viking times to modern digital payments.

Think of Denmark performing as a tightrope walker who balances skillfully on a rope with the sign "Economic Stability". Denmark's monetary policy balances between their national currency and economic alignment with Europe through their dual grip of the "Krone" and a "Euro Peg" marked pole. This balancing act represents Denmark's unique monetary policy: Denmark runs its own national currency while preserving a close connection to the Euro.

Denmark decided not to enter the Eurozone's lively circus tent to adopt the euro but instead established its own small yet secure booth beside it. They watch Eurozone movements behind their curtains and adjust their krone to echo the euro's pace. The "ERM II" mechanism keeps the Danish krone closely aligned with the euro to maintain a consistent and stable economic environment.

The krone and euro move together like dance partners performing in perfect sync. Denmark meticulously synchronizes its monetary actions to follow the Eurozone's lead in establishing monetary policy direction. This "fixed exchange rate regime" operates like a precise waltz routine which reduces unexpected movements and maintains consistent predictable steps.

Denmark's booth benefits from several advantages through this intimate economic connection.

Trade Harmony: Trade interactions with Eurozone neighbors progress smoothly like an expertly coordinated duet because exchange rate variability does not create any disruptions. Danish businesses enjoy secure export opportunities while consumers purchase imported products without worrying about unexpected price increases.
Price Stability: The Eurozone's rigorous inflation control acts as a harmonious tune which prevents price spikes from occurring in Denmark. The economy operates smoothly under the guidance of a dependable conductor who keeps all financial elements aligned.
Investor Confidence: Denmark enjoys the benefits of the Eurozone's respected reputation by drawing investors who value the krone's steady nature.

The synchronized economic performance between Denmark and the Eurozone faces certain constraints.

Limited Solo Performances: The Danish central bank must operate within strict boundaries like a musician who cannot stray from the prescribed orchestra score when managing its monetary policy. Denmark must mirror the Eurozone's actions to keep its economic equilibrium intact.
Vulnerability to External Shocks: Any unexpected turmoil within the Eurozone will unavoidably impact Denmark due to their strong connection. The dependence places them at risk from economic developments that they cannot manage.

Denmark has to maintain its economic stability through a continuous delicate balancing act which demands ongoing monitoring and precise adjustments. It's a trade-off: Denmark exchanges monetary independence to gain stable economic conditions through its strong connection to the euro.

Denmark's skillful management of its economic balance has shown remarkable success. Denmark successfully steered through economic challenges while preserving their distinctive stance in the European Union. It is uncertain whether Denmark will persist in its current balancing act forever or join the Eurozone completely. Denmark maintains its elegant balance on a narrow economic tightrope through skillful fiscal strategies.

The Little Mermaid's Kingdom: Where Money Talks, but Nobody Shouts

Envision a place from fairy tales where people live by hygge principles and the tax collector smiles. Denmark stands as a compact kingdom that combines generosity with substantial wealth. The Danish krone operates independently yet remains vigilant of the euro's influence. The Danish krone executes a sophisticated monetary dance like a waltz which ensures trade stability and smooth operations with European partners.

The image of Denmark extends beyond its currency and the cozy fireside evenings. Denmark functions as a welfare state where the government distributes benefits to its people like a fairy godmother sprinkling magic dust. Free healthcare? Check. Free education from kindergarten to university? Check. The Danish welfare state offers generous unemployment benefits and parental leave that would earn panda approval. Check, check, check!

The term "flexicurity" seems like a creative invention from a jazz musician who dabbles in economics. This system allows businesses to hire and fire with Lego-like precision while workers benefit from a safety net crafted from unicorn hair and rainbows. Trust between employers and employees functions like a high-wire act that maintains a delicate balance yet functions successfully.

The Krone's Humble Hum

Although the Danish krone lacks the visual appeal of other currencies it serves as Denmark's economic foundation. Denmark maintains control over inflation and import prices through its euro-pegged krone which functions like a dependable guardian protecting the castle gates. Denmark maintains financial flexibility through its currency which enables precise adjustments to interest rates and the ability to address economic troubles with agility that would earn Hans Christian Andersen's admiration.

While some believe Denmark should abandon the krone to join the euro system others think Danes value their financial independence as much as a child values their favorite teddy bear. Control over economic decisions during turbulent times is something they value. The debate simmers quietly like gløgg boiling on a frosty night but currently the krone stands as the dominant currency.

The Welfare State: The Danish welfare state functions as a comforting embrace to all citizens but demands a significant financial commitment.

The Danish welfare state feels like a comforting embrace during a chilly day, yet it demands a considerable financial sacrifice. Danes willingly pay high taxes despite their substantial income because they view it as necessary for maintaining their ideal social system. They believe in the worth of a system which provides universal access to healthcare and education and offers a safety net for everyone because it relies on mutual trust and shared responsibility.

But even fairy tales have their challenges. The aging population in Denmark operates like a countdown clock since fewer people contribute to the system while more retirees receive its benefits. Creative solutions must address the challenge by raising the retirement age and increasing workforce participation. The process of globalization presents challenges because it lures companies to shift their operations to nations that offer lower tax rates.

Denmark's Economic Dance: More Than Just a Waltz

Denmark's economy isn't just surviving, it's thriving! This region stands as a beacon of innovative spirit where green technology and wind energy flourish while small businesses experience explosive growth akin to wildflowers in a field. Through the "flexicurity" model businesses gain flexibility to navigate economic turbulence while employees stay protected knowing they won't face unemployment.

The essence of our system goes beyond numerical data and graphical representations. This approach focuses on human potential by building a society that offers every individual an opportunity for success. Visualize a Danish youngster who has escaped student debt burdens while benefiting from accessible healthcare and a reliable safety net for life's unexpected setbacks. This system encourages creative pursuits and entrepreneurial spirit while enabling individuals to chase their aspirations with the security of not slipping into hardship.

Looking Ahead: A Fairy Tale with a Twist

Denmark's future appears promising but still faces multiple challenges. Economic stability requires constant vigilance and adaptation because of demographic aging along with worldwide competition plus potential economic downturns. Denmark stands as a country where innovation meets collaboration and dreams thrive alongside a strong community belief system and readiness to adopt change.

Danish krone will maintain its relationship with the euro while Denmark's welfare system transforms itself to address emerging challenges and the Danish population will keep developing a society that thrives both economically and morally. This story functions as a fairy tale with a modern twist and illustrates both economic growth and social responsibility while demonstrating human creativity and the continuous hope for an improved future.

The Danish krone stands before a critical junction where its path forward includes both thrilling opportunities and tough choices. Visualize the krone as a Viking ship navigating unknown seas.

1. The Digital Krone: A New Kind of Ship

The primary challenge facing development teams is whether to design and construct an entirely new class of vessel which would be known as the e-krone. The digital vessel would serve as a modern yacht running on cutting-edge technology. The e-krone concept offers quicker transaction processing along with expanded financial access and innovative breakthroughs. This new digital currency brings serious questions about personal privacy protection and security as well as potential effects on established banking institutions.

Danmarks Nationalbank is thoroughly evaluating the plans for the e-krone to understand its advantages and potential dangers prior to deployment. They function as shipbuilders who carefully design and test their vessels to prove they can withstand the digital economy's vast ocean.

2. Regional Cooperation: Sailing Together

Denmark isn't navigating these waters alone. Denmark sails together with other Nordic countries toward their common future. Regional cooperation functions as a powerful wind that propels the krone forward with stability and strength.

These countries can survive economic challenges together while enhancing trade and investment and addressing shared issues such as climate change. They can strengthen their influence in the European Union while making sure their interests receive attention. These Nordic countries operate like a formidable Viking fleet with significant power and authority across European waters.

3. The European Question: Choosing a Course

The krone faces the pivotal decision of whether to become part of the eurozone which operates as a massive fleet using the euro. The decision amounts to either remaining aboard their own well-known vessel or merging with a greater fleet that holds more power.

Adopting the euro leads to more efficient trading practices while reducing expenses and increasing influence in European matters. This choice requires surrendering a degree of sovereignty comparable to a captain yielding control to a governing power.

Denmark has chosen to maintain its national currency but has connected it to the euro through a fixed exchange rate system similar to a small boat being anchored to a larger ship. The arrangement delivers stability yet restricts their ability to operate independently.

The intense debate persists as both sides present fervent arguments. The eurozone appears to be a protective haven for some people but represents a loss of autonomy to others in a massive, faceless armada. The Danish voters will determine through a referendum the future direction of the krone.

The Krone's Journey: A Path of Exploration

The krone will face an exciting yet unpredictable journey ahead. Whether it embraces the digital revolution, strengthens regional ties, or joins the eurozone, one thing is certain: The krone will remain an active participant in the global economy as it navigates emerging challenges while steering towards a brighter economic future.

The Norwegian Krone: Oil Wealth, Economic Resilience, and a Nordic Model

The Krone's Saga: A Narrative of National Identity, Oil Exploration, and Shrewd Governing Practices

A freshly printed young krone emerges from the printing press as its crisp paper vibrates with untapped potential. The krone came into existence in 1875 when it became part of the dynamic Scandinavian Monetary Union. Standing alongside its Swedish and Danish relatives gave the krone a sense of belonging and unity. Borders were crossed with cheerful trade movements while fishermen traded their catches without difficulty and families enjoyed worry-free vacations due to uncomplicated exchange rates. The krone possessed genuine worth during those times because its value was firmly attached to precious metal.

Any well-crafted saga would eventually encounter its share of challenges. The Great Wars swept across the globe which resulted in damage to the previously flawless surface of the krone. As countries faced financial pressures from warfare, they abandoned the traditional gold standard which previously served as a reliable foundation. Uncertainty shook the krone causing its value to oscillate like a vessel amidst turbulent waters. The family that once stood together began to separate as each member individually faced their own storm.

Despite its battered state the krone emerged from turmoil with a strong sense of identity. The krone longed to regain its stability and recapture the tranquil times from its early existence. For a short time it attached itself to the US dollar which served as a strong life preserver throughout the stormy waters of the post-war global landscape. But fate, it seemed, had other plans.

The discovery of oil in the North Sea unleashed a stream of black gold that altered the krone's future. The powerful industrial resource known as oil flowed through Norway while the krone evolved from a simple worker to a wealthy entity. Its value shot up to unprecedented heights attracting global admiration.

But with great wealth came great responsibility. Although the krone was young, it possessed an understanding of the dangers of unexpected wealth. The krone observed how other currencies fell victim to the "Dutch disease" which caused their economies to decay as abandoned gardens would. Norway followed an alternative route with the krone leading the way.

Norway established the Oil Fund as a massive savings account for its future. The krone remembered its historical challenges and chose to maintain savings for future needs by strategically investing oil revenue internationally and developing a diverse financial portfolio through careful management.

The krone represents Norway's determined spirit and shrewd planning as it stands strong today. The krone moves freely throughout international markets and its worth mirrors the careful decisions made by Norway. The Norwegian krone serves as the standard cash for daily purchases and becomes a symbol for future aspirations for its citizens. This legacy shows how a nation faced many difficulties yet accumulated resources wisely to guarantee its economic stability for future generations.

But the saga doesn't end here. The krone remains alert and expects upcoming challenges on its path. Digital currencies suggest a forthcoming cashless world while global economic conditions demonstrate the same unpredictability as the North Sea. The strength of the krone combined with its prudent management prepares it for any upcoming challenges while guaranteeing Norway's bright future under the midnight sun.

The value of the Norwegian krone behaves like a kite which flies on the powerful gusts created by changes in oil prices. The krone ascends when oil prices rise but plummets when oil prices drop. The experience provides excitement but carries inherent dangers.

Norway functions as a Viking ship where petrodollars fill the sails. The exchange of dollars for kroner generates demand which results in an increase in the krone's value. The "Dutch Disease" curse aboard Norway's powerful ship renders its other products like fine handcrafted furniture and stunning fjord tours too costly for international buyers.

Norway, however, is no ordinary Viking. The Government Pension Fund Global operates as a massive reserve for oil money which Norway has invested strategically worldwide. Norway sends ravens to collect distant riches which prevents the krone from strengthening and maintains the Viking ship's equilibrium.

This fund exemplifies visionary long-term investment strategies. The fund acts as a seed which develops into a strong oak tree that provides protection and benefits to future generations. But even this oak faces challenges. As climate change continues to advance Norway must steer towards a sustainable future through strategic investment shifts to renewable energy sources.

The fund operates as a gigantic force whose steps make noticeable impacts throughout the international marketplace. Observers monitor its actions while experts analyze its investment strategies. Norway bears a profound duty as a wise elder understands because its choices influence both its own destiny and the entire world.

The krone's movements remain in flux as it reacts to changes in the oil market alongside the fund's guiding influence and global economic fluctuations. This narrative demonstrates how calculated planning and foresight can guide us to prosperity despite the unpredictable nature of global markets and the uncertainty of future events.

Norway's Krone, Model, and Green Tightrope demonstrate its challenging balancing act

Norway is a fascinating case study. Norway has achieved remarkable wealth status among nations. The country's wealth originates from its abundant oil and gas reserves. Norway has not squandered its entire financial resources. The nation has established a robust social safety net system. The country has taken a leading position worldwide in terms of environmental sustainability. Norway's currency (the krone) interacts with its distinctive economic and social system (the "Norwegian Model") and its environmental goals in a complicated way that is continuously changing.

The Krone: More Than Just Oil Money?

Norway uses the Norwegian Krone (NOK) as its national currency. Its value is influenced by many factors. Oil prices stand out as a crucial factor. The value of the krone strengthens when global oil prices reach high levels. Norway's status as a significant oil exporter explains this. But it's not just about oil. The interest rates established by Norges Bank (the central bank of Norway) are influential. Global economic conditions influence the entire financial system. The stability of Norway generates investor confidence which is another important factor.

The krone experiences fascinating pressures during the year 2025. The international push toward renewable energy sources produces economic uncertainty. The world is changing fast. There's a push for renewable energy. Long-term demand for Norway's oil and gas production may experience changes as a result of this situation. Norges Bank monitors inflation in a manner consistent with central banks globally. They're trying to keep the economy stable. By adjusting interest rates they try to maintain economic stability. This, in turn, affects the krone's value.

No other currency pegs to the krone. It floats freely. Market conditions determine its value fluctuations. This can be good and bad. When the krone weakens it enhances the competitiveness of Norwegian exports excluding oil. A stronger krone can make imports cheaper. It's a constant balancing act.

The Norwegian Model: A Safety Net and Shared Success

The "Norwegian Model" refers to Norway's distinctive economic approach. This system operates as a free market economy while simultaneously providing extensive welfare benefits. High taxation funds extensive social support programs in this system. The Norwegian Model includes universal healthcare together with generous parental leave benefits and strong unemployment support.

Key features of the Norwegian Model include:

Tripartite Cooperation: The government together with employers' organizations and labor unions engage in close collaboration. They negotiate wages and working

conditions. This approach reduces workplace disputes while establishing common goals among all parties.
High Degree of Trust: Norwegians generally trust their government and institutions. The model requires this feature to function properly. The public demonstrates their willingness to pay elevated taxes when they observe the benefits that result from it. They believe the system is fair.
Egalitarianism: The disparity between Norway's wealthy individuals and poor citizens remains minimal. The small income gap in Norway results partly from the progressive tax system. The cultural focus on equality contributes to this outcome.
Strong Social Safety Net: The welfare state establishes a protective safety net accessible to all citizens. This reduces poverty and inequality. The system provides people with enough security to undertake ventures such as opening new businesses.
Soverign Wealth Fund. The Norwegian government stores the majority of its oil-generated income.

The Green Shift: A Challenge and an Opportunity

Norway stands as one of the principal producers of oil and gas. The country has dedicated itself to decreasing its carbon footprint. This is a huge challenge. The situation demands achieving two conflicting objectives at once.

The country has set ambitious climate goals. The nation has set a target to achieve low emissions by the year 2050. The nation is heavily allocating funds toward renewable energy sources such as hydropower and wind power. Norway stands out as one of the leading countries in the adoption of electric vehicles. Electric cars are very popular in Norway. This is partly due to government incentives.

The Government Pension Fund Global which is frequently referred to as the "Oil Fund" serves as a critical component in this narrative. Norway places its oil revenue savings into this location. This fund stands as one of the biggest sovereign wealth funds globally. The fund is now more focused than ever on investments that promote sustainability. It's divesting from some fossil fuel companies. It's investing in renewable energy projects.

However, the transition isn't easy. Experts continue to discuss the potential directions for the oil and gas industry moving forward. A group of people support the immediate phase-out of this sector. There are people who believe that oil and gas remain essential for maintaining energy security. And that it provides jobs and revenue.

Balancing the Books: Economic Growth vs. Social and Environmental Goals

This is the heart of the matter. How does Norway maintain its economic success built on oil wealth while upholding its social and environmental responsibilities?

It's a constant negotiation. There are trade-offs. The increased operating costs for companies result from the implementation of stricter environmental regulations. This could impact jobs and economic growth. The consequences of failing to act on climate change could prove even more destructive in the long run.

The Norwegian Model proves beneficial because it prioritizes cooperation and consensus. The government works to gather all relevant parties for discussions. They work together to identify difficulties and create solutions. This doesn't mean there aren't disagreements. This approach provides a structured method to identify shared interests.

Challenges in 2025 and Beyond:

Global Energy Transition: No one can predict how quickly or broadly the world will reduce its reliance on fossil fuels because this remains a significant unknown factor. How will this affect Norway's economy? How will it affect the krone?
Maintaining Competitiveness: Norway is a high-cost country. Norway must sustain its competitiveness within the globalized marketplace. This means investing in innovation and education.
Aging Population: Norway shares the trait of an aging population with other developed nations. This puts pressure on the welfare state. The working-age population will diminish as the number of retirees continues to grow.
Inequality (Even in Norway): Despite being a relatively equal society Norway still faces issues with inequality. People discuss strategies to distribute Norway's wealth so that all citizens gain from it.
Geopolitical Uncertainty: Multiple global events including the war in Ukraine have generated uncertainty. The war in Ukraine along with other global events could have consequences for both the krone and Norway's economy.
Maintaining its high trust environment.

The Human Side of the Equation:

Numbers and policy details can easily obscure understanding. We should not forget about the human experiences that are part of this story.

Think of the oil worker in Stavanger. The oil worker from Stavanger faces uncertainty about his job security because the world is shifting away from fossil fuels. Think of the young entrepreneur in Oslo. She could be enthusiastic about the possibilities presented by the green economy.

Think of the family in rural Norway. The family in rural Norway likely receives support from their robust social safety net.

The decisions made in Oslo directly impact these individuals. These people experience the transition period as they live through it now. The equation includes the hopes, fears and aspirations of these people.

The Future: A Sustainable Path?

Norway is working to establish a route towards environmental sustainability. It's not an easy path. There are many challenges. But Norway has some advantages. It has a strong economy. It has a well-educated population. It has a tradition of social cooperation. The country has made environmental sustainability one of its core commitments.

The monetary unit krone together with the Norwegian Model and the green transition demonstrate interrelated connections. The krone, the Norwegian Model and the green transition together form one complete narrative. This narrative explores how one nation is attempting to maintain prosperity while promoting social justice and environmental responsibility. The story continues to develop. The story of success depends on multiple different variables. The success story relies on international factors beyond Norway's control.

In this envisioned world money transforms into digital energy which flows directly from Norway's central financial system instead of being stored in bank accounts. The digital krone represents Norway's ambitious vision for transforming money into the future.

Think of it like this: cash, but with a digital heartbeat. No more crumpled bills or jingling coins. The digital currency would securely live on your phone as an invisible asset that you can spend using a simple tap on the screen.

What motivates Norway to explore this digital krone when it already dominates cashless payment systems? Imagine your preferred payment application disappearing overnight. The digital krone acts as a financial backup allowing you to make essential purchases and sustain economic stability.

It's not just about convenience. The digital krone offers a platform for innovation that will lead to financial services beyond our current comprehension. Imagine financial solutions including micro-payments for digital content alongside automated saving mechanisms and currency programs that automatically process your bill payments.

The digital krone serves as a crucial tool for seniors and bank account-less individuals to engage with the modern economy through its simple and accessible digital platform.

But this isn't just a Norwegian story. It's a global saga. The digital yuan from China has generated significant attention while the Eurozone follows closely behind. The innovative spirit of Norway prevents it from falling behind in today's technological advancements.

A digital krone requires overcoming numerous challenges before it can be established. What strategies can we implement to maintain privacy protection within our digital environment? What measures can we implement to protect the system from cyberattacks? The introduction of digital currency will change the financial landscape.

Norges Bank faces these challenges as Norway's central bank. Through intensive research and public engagement they work to make the digital krone advantageous for every Norwegian citizen.

The digital krone represents a new currency for Norway while symbolizing its economic progress and innovation. The digital krone represents Norway's steadfast commitment to steer through the unpredictable shifts of today's global economy. Their work demonstrates strong dedication to innovative approaches along with inclusive practices and enduring strength.

Norway stands prepared for the digital future of currency. Are you?

The Czech Koruna: A Currency of Transition, Integration, and European Aspirations

The Austro-Hungarian krone served as the empire's common currency and was under the administration of the Austro-Hungarian Bank which received joint control from both Austria and Hungary. The Austro-Hungarian Empire's stability collapsed because of World War I which caused significant damage to the krone. The wartime monetary expansion resulted in severe inflation and reduced confidence in the currency.

Czechoslovakia gained independence in 1918 while taking over a failing monetary system. The previous krone currency became unsuitable and a fresh independent currency became necessary both to secure economic independence and to mark the departure from imperial rule.

The first action taken to establish Czechoslovak monetary independence involved overprinting banknotes with a distinctive Czechoslovak insignia which served as transitional money. This provisional currency solution allowed time for designing a new monetary system while identifying the money in circulation in the new country.

The inaugural Czechoslovak Minister of Finance Alois Rašín rose to prominence as a vital player. He advocated fiscal discipline and recognized that economic health depended on maintaining a robust currency.

Rašín made a vital decision when he decided to physically separate Czechoslovak currency from the currencies of other successor states. The government implemented a policy where only banknotes it stamped within national borders were accepted as legal tender. This challenging policy led to temporary economic struggles yet proved essential for the formation of the new state.

In 1919 the Czechoslovak koruna (Kč) became the official currency as it took over from the previously stamped banknotes. The new republic created banknotes and coins that showcased national symbols to represent its identity.

The koruna experienced challenging beginnings due to persistent inflation risks. Despite facing controversy Rašín's policies proved effective when the koruna achieved gradual stabilization.

The Ministry of Finance's Banking Office initially managed currency operations while performing central bank functions. The National Bank of Czechoslovakia became a fully independent central bank in 1926.

The accumulation of gold reserves played a fundamental role in supporting the koruna's value and establishing trust. Czechoslovakia made significant efforts to accumulate gold reserves by utilizing loans and trade surpluses.

Czechoslovakia turned to foreign nations for loans as a means to fund its economy and support its new currency system.

The koruna achieved stability and earned regional respect by the mid-1920s while representing the economic triumph of the new republic.

Introducing the koruna demonstrated the country's commitment to achieving long-term economic stability and prosperity. The creation of the koruna played a crucial role in establishing Czechoslovakia's independence and represented much more than monetary value.

The history of the koruna persists through the division of the country. The koruna's legacy endures as a symbol of nation-building challenges and achievements alongside a sound currency despite both Czechia and Slovakia joining the euro zone.

The initial period demonstrated the critical role of effective leadership alongside the requirement for reliable monetary policies and the lasting connection between national identity and currency. The koruna played a critical role in Czechoslovakia's development and continues to represent the nation's historical period.

Imagine a world where money doesn't talk. The currency remains silent about market forces and economic trends. The currency moves as one with the government, functioning as a quiet defender in a centrally controlled economic system. The Czechoslovak koruna (Kčs) functioned under strict government control throughout the communist era.

The Czechoslovak koruna served as a captive currency controlled by the state from 1948 until 1989. Prices? Official authorities established prices without considering resource scarcity issues. Fancy a new car? Get in line together with your fellow comrades and trust that the factory will receive its planned production targets. Thinking about exchanging your koruna for dollars to travel West? The Iron Curtain functioned as both a political and monetary barrier during its existence.

The koruna functioned as a bird trapped within a luxurious cage. The koruna could move freely inside the planned economic system yet faced severe restrictions whenever it tried to transcend those boundaries. Western trade operated at minimal levels and the official exchange rates were fictional narratives that did not represent the koruna's actual worth on the black market.

This monetary isolation was a double-edged sword. The Czechoslovak economy received protection from global competition through this system but simultaneously suffered from limited innovation and reduced efficiency. The koruna thrived under artificial conditions yet its development suffered due to limited exposure to fresh air and sunlight.

The year 1989 brought the Velvet Revolution which toppled the existing system while initiating the disorderly emergence of a market economy. The koruna found itself thrust onto an unfamiliar stage without any preparation. The price controls disappeared and inflation spiked while the currency experienced a freefall towards the bottom. The state-owned enterprises which once supported the economy collapsed because of competitive pressures resulting in widespread unemployment.

The currency experienced a brutal introduction to new realities after being confined to central planning for decades. The transition faced numerous difficulties but brought about emancipation. The koruna became liberated to determine its own worth within the dynamic marketplace after years of state control.

The koruna's history during communist rule serves as a lesson on governmental economic control against humanity's persistent pursuit of freedom. Money fundamentally represents the characteristics of the society which utilizes it. If a society builds its foundation on oppression and artificiality its currency will display inevitable signs of damage.

The Czech Koruna stands as a young explorer ready to discover the European Union's expansive realm. The Czech Republic's entry into the EU in 2004 served as their gateway to a new world of prospects and difficulties. The Koruna rejected the Euro's allure and maintained its separate identity to preserve its independent status.

This journey hasn't been without its bumps. The Koruna learned essential rules of financial conduct known as the "convergence criteria" which required control over inflation and stability in currency value. The Koruna needed to adjust its driving habits to operate on the right side of the road because it was accustomed to the left side.

Maintaining competitiveness remains a complex challenge for the Koruna. A weaker Koruna acts as a favorable tailwind by making Czech exports more affordable which helps local businesses grow. A weaker Koruna creates higher prices for imported goods which act as a headwind pushing expenses up for everyday Czech citizens. The currency operates as a tightrope walker who must maintain stability between encouraging exports and maintaining domestic price stability.

And then there's the big question looming over the Koruna's adventure: The Koruna stands before a decision about whether it should exchange its current currency status for adoption of the Euro. This choice carries significant consequences similar to deciding between joining an EU tour group or traveling independently.

The Euro provides benefits for travel and commerce through seamless movement without border stops. The Euro provides a stable environment that could draw new investors similarly to how tourist destinations attract visitors. Choosing to adopt the Euro involves forfeiting national control which is similar to giving someone else your map. The adoption of the Euro may result in a slower response to financial disruptions and lead to concerns about eroding the Koruna's distinct character as it becomes like wearing standard-issue attire.

The Czech people are divided. A portion of the population supports the adoption of the Euro because they believe it will bring increased prosperity and a sense of connection. Some individuals maintain strong support for the Koruna because they regard it as a representation of their achieved independence and protection from outside disturbances.

The Czech National Bank acts as a vigilant protector to ensure the safe passage of the Koruna throughout its monetary path. The Czech National Bank closely monitors economic conditions to maintain the Koruna's stability while setting preparations in motion for future Euro adoption.

The future remains unpredictable with its serpentine path filled with unexpected changes. Does the Koruna stand to exchange its currency status for Euro membership someday or will it pursue its solitary financial path? Only time will tell. But one thing is certain: The history of the Koruna mirrors the Czech Republic's narrative of merging its national identity with European integration while valuing both progress and tradition. The Czech people continue to write this ongoing story.

The Czech koruna stands strong like a resilient ship amidst a dynamic sea of transformations. A transformed world surrounds the Czech koruna as it navigates the currents of technological advancement alongside global cooperation winds with intermittent European Union turbulence.

A digital koruna represents one of the most significant upcoming changes on the financial horizon. You have digital money transferred directly from the Czech National Bank to your phone instead of dealing with bulky coins or paper banknotes. With this system you have immediate access to the financial source. This Central Bank Digital Currency, also known as CBDC, promises to deliver extremely fast transactions at minimal costs while providing banking access to underserved populations.

But hold on! As we prepare to embark on the digital currency journey we must navigate several potential dangers. Privacy is a big one. No one wishes to have their entire buying history monitored continuously. Those digital pirates known as hackers could pose significant threats. The Czech National Bank approaches their operations with increased vigilance and precision similar to how a veteran captain navigates dangerous seas. Research teams are looking at Sweden and China to understand their approaches to these issues.

You might wonder why we should consider the digital koruna. You never have to search for cards or cash again when you pay for groceries with just a quick smartphone tap. Transferring funds to family members living overseas would become both efficient and cost-effective. Financial innovation in the Czech Republic could flourish under this new system which would also generate new employment opportunities and strengthen economic growth.

All worthwhile adventures come with their share of risks. The big question remains whether people will accept and trust this innovative digital currency. The Czech National Bank understands that they must guide people throughout this process by providing clear explanations and fostering trust.

And the Czech Republic isn't sailing alone! The Czech Republic operates as a member of a regional team with their Central European neighbors who are particularly joined by the Visegrád Group acting as dependable partners. The team distributes maps, exchanges observations and ensures that all members follow the planned path.

The European Union stands as an immense and erratic sea. The Czech Republic stands alone as a ship that sails with a massive fleet yet determines its own path. The Czech Republic uses its own currency called the koruna that navigates independently on market currents while other countries use currencies that are linked to the euro. Czech citizens and politicians regularly argue about whether they should adopt the euro or maintain their independence.

Global transformations continue to accelerate at an unprecedented rate. Global shockwaves from the Ukraine war combined with universal battles against inflation have created widespread economic challenges. The Czech National Bank acts as a watchful sentinel who monitors for potential dangers while maintaining control of the economic direction.

While many focus on numbers and charts during these turbulent times it remains crucial to understand that the koruna represents people. It's about families, businesses, and everyday lives. The Czech National Bank understands their mission and works diligently to establish policies that protect everyone's savings while building a strong economic foundation that enables prosperity for all citizens.

So, what's the future of the koruna? The path ahead contains potential for growth but also presents obstacles and chances for advancement. The journey involves adopting innovative technologies while collaborating with partners and maneuvering through complicated global dynamics. The koruna stands prepared to embark on its 21st-century voyage and beyond through meticulous planning, bravery, and tremendous resilience.

The Armenian Dram: A Currency of Independence, Resilience, and Regional Challenges

During Soviet rule Armenia used the Soviet ruble as its official currency. Following its independence in 1991 Armenia introduced the dram as its national currency in 1993 to replace the Soviet ruble. Multiple factors created challenges during the transition period including the Nagorno-Karabakh War along with economic blockades and the Soviet system's collapse coupled with market economy adoption. A combination of factors resulted in hyperinflation that severely depreciated the dram and brought economic difficulty to Armenian citizens. The government introduced stabilization measures that incorporated tight monetary policies along with fiscal discipline and structural reforms and sought foreign aid to stabilize the dram and control inflation. The dram functions as a stable currency that demonstrates the resilience and progress of Armenia. Armenia's economic progress depends on maintaining the stability of its currency during current difficulties.

Armenia's dram represents a powerful symbol of endurance despite its small size. It has endured ongoing adversity while being pummeled by the turbulent Nagorno-Karabakh conflict. The struggle between Armenia and its neighbors over territorial control and national identity has impacted both Armenia's geographical boundaries and economic environment.

A young Armenian entrepreneur driven by dreams and ambition attempts to establish a business while facing the unpredictability created by ongoing conflict. Entrepreneurs celebrate obtaining critical funding one day only to face the challenge of safeguarding their assets against the repercussions of renewed fighting the next. Many Armenians live with the relentless fear that their hard-earned achievements might vanish instantly.

The ongoing conflict acts as an unending wave that slowly destroys economic stability's core structure. The defense spending drains essential resources which could have been used for education and healthcare. Trade route disruptions pose significant challenges for business success. The presence of conflict forces investors to search for more secure places to park their capital. The conflict causes a devastating brain drain because gifted young individuals depart to find better security elsewhere.

Both the dram and the Armenian people have demonstrated extraordinary endurance when facing these challenges. But resilience alone is not enough. Armenia's true prosperity depends on establishing long-term peace which will foster economic growth and enable its citizens to flourish.

Picture a future where war's remnants give way to factory activity, Armenian refugees return to rebuild their homeland and the dram emerges as a marker of stability and economic development. The hope that drives Armenian perseverance shapes their ability to endure even the toughest challenges.

The narrative extends beyond a simple tale of war and suffering. The narrative demonstrates how people show determination in building brighter futures for both themselves and their offspring. The narrative celebrates the Armenian people's unbreakable spirit which will eventually overcome all obstacles.

Armenia resembles a professional tightrope walker while maintaining its position on the narrow path of the Eurasian Economic Union (EEU). The allure of the Russian market and its trade opportunities attracts businesses from all over. The dangers of becoming too dependent on a stronger neighbor form a significant threat.

Following its entry into the EEU in 2015 Armenia has developed intricate economic relationships with its partners which involve particularly complex dynamics with Russia. The Armenian dram behaves as a steadfast follower of the powerful Russian ruble. Armenia's dram currency reaches its peak performance when the Russian ruble maintains strength because of increased trade activities and remittances sent back by Armenians working in Russia. When the ruble loses its strength, the dram suffers because exports grow more expensive and economic uncertainty creates a pervasive shadow.

Membership in the EEU has created significant opportunities for Armenia. Picturing thriving marketplaces where Armenian enterprises exhibit their superb wines, brandies, and artisanal products to enthusiastic purchasers from throughout the union. Armenian workers take advantage of labor mobility to find superior opportunities in bordering nations and send important money transfers to their home country.

Armenia's economic partnership brings financial drawbacks. Armenia remains exposed to Russia's economic challenges and political decisions due to its reliance on Russia. Economic penalties against Russia send shockwaves through Armenia's financial landscape which leads to trade blockages and investment declines.

Armenia understands the importance of expanding its economic connections outside of the EEU to protect its financial stability. Armenia is building new partnerships with the European Union while investigating promising opportunities in Asia's rapidly expanding markets. Armenia behaves like a dedicated scholar gaining insights from EU experiences while pursuing investments from Eastern technology powerhouses.

Armenia encounters multiple challenges while pursuing a diversified economic pathway. Economic headwinds develop due to global uncertainties such as Ukraine's continuing conflict. The unrelenting beast of inflation eats away at the dram's purchasing power, creating financial difficulties for Armenian businesses and general citizens.

The Central Bank of Armenia operates as the diligent protector of the dram through its monetary policy measures to control inflation and sustain financial stability. The Central Bank of Armenia acts as an adept conductor who directs the economy towards a stable performance.

The future of Armenia's economy depends on its success in achieving a careful equilibrium. Armenia needs to develop its EEU connections while building new partnerships and creating an investment-friendly atmosphere to draw international capital.

Armenia emerges as a vibrant tapestry that integrates threads of tradition together with strands of innovation. The nation achieves success by leveraging its distinctive advantages including its deep cultural roots and expanding tech industry as it manages the challenges of globalization.

Armenia navigates the complex world of economics and geopolitics through resilience and adaptation while relentlessly chasing prosperity.

The Dram's Dance: The Dram's Dance presents A Digital Duet with Destiny (A Glimpse into 2025).

Armenia emerges as a dynamic tapestry that blends timeless traditions with contemporary ambitions while its heart pulses alongside the beat of the Dram. This digital Dram represents a new era of currency that transcends traditional ways of being secretly held in wallets and exchanged with silent understanding. A digital Dram dances on the stage of innovation with its dynamic movements.

The Digital Dram: A Leap of Faith

Picture this: A Yerevan entrepreneur who radiates ambition uses digital currency to instantly send Drams to her grandmother living in a mountain village. End the wait times for money transfers and eliminate the expensive transaction fees that diminish available funds. A Central Bank Digital Currency (CBDC) represents a digital Dram that will flow effortlessly throughout all parts of Armenia's economic system.

Through diligent leadership the Central Bank of Armenia (CBA) directs the harmonious development of digital currency. Experts are thoroughly analyzing the score to ensure security and privacy become dominant themes in the lives of the people rather than secondary notes.

Picture a digital dance floor where transactions move effortlessly at unprecedented speed and cost efficiency. Armenian small businesses which constitute the nation's economic core now perform their operations more agilely thanks to reduced costs. The digital Dram eradicates the darkness where illegal activities once thrived by illuminating each transaction.

But this dance isn't without its challenges. Access to the digital stage remains out of reach for some people. Certain individuals are unable to participate because they don't possess smartphones or internet access. Digital literacy must be transformed into a shared language through the careful guidance of the CBA which acts like a patient dance instructor teaching hesitant steps.

The Diaspora: A Global Chorus

The Armenian diaspora creates a worldwide chorus that connects generations through music from Los Angeles to Paris. The collective voices of the diaspora combine into a symphonic expression of financial support and cultural pride which reaches back to their ancestral homeland.

What appear to be simple exchanges of money are heartfelt messages in Drams that support families and enable dreams while connecting distant nations. As skilled choreographers perform on stage, diaspora investors deliver their knowledge and financial resources to generate employment opportunities and stimulate innovation.

The Armenian government acknowledges this powerful harmony and is treating investors like honored guests. Armenia becomes a land of opportunity as investment incentives shine and bureaucratic hurdles dissolve. The partnership stands as a tango combining both shared heritage and common future goals.

Sustainable Growth: A Harmonious Ballet

Amidst the global stage of uncertainty Armenia embarks on a dance towards sustainable growth. The performance involves multiple participants working together as economic diversification shares the stage with education and environmental responsibility.

Envision a future where technology merges with tourism and renewable energy to perform their perfect synchronized pirouette. STEM education alongside an innovative mindset enables young people to make strides into a more promising future. Both local and foreign investors find their way to a business environment that stands out for its transparency and efficiency.

The ballet serves as a tribute to Armenia's stunning natural beauty while its landscapes provide a spectacular background. Solar panels sparkle like gemstones across the hills while wind turbines spin through elegant curves as nature delivers its applause.

The Human Touch: The Heart of the Performance

The dazzling choreography and soaring music obscures the true heart of the performance which is the Armenian people. The genuine essence of this dance stems from their dreams and their aspirations together with their resilience.

The performance remains stable and confident through the consistent presence of a strong Dram in both physical and digital forms. Through diaspora engagement Armenians experience a heartfelt connection that spans multiple continents. The potential for sustainable growth creates a future in which every individual has the opportunity to succeed.

Facing the Future, En Pointe

Armenia may be geographically limited but it commands a significant presence in global affairs. Armenia stands poised as a nation of dancers who will confront their future with grace and precision. Armenia faces difficult challenges but each elegant jump and meticulously planned move brings it nearer to fulfilling its dreams.

The Dram serves as a musical guide for this journey in all its manifestations. This stands as evidence of innovative spirit combined with diaspora support and sustainable development commitment. This narrative represents Armenia's unyielding spirit through the symphony of hope and the dance of progress.

The South African Rand: A Currency of Transformation, Inequality, and Continental Ambitions

The South African Rand: A Currency Forged in Struggle and Hope

The South African Rand functions beyond money circulation as a durable emblem representing the nation's challenging history. The Rand emerged during apartheid and has reflected South Africa's achievements and challenges throughout its journey toward democracy.

1961: A New Currency, A Divided Nation

The introduction of the Rand coincided with South Africa's transition to a republic and departure from the Commonwealth in 1961 during a period when the country bore deep apartheid scars. The racial segregation system harshly subjugated the Black majority while leaving a dark legacy for the nation's development.

When the Rand took over from the South African pound it showed a false strength because one Rand traded at 1.40 US dollars. The economic façade concealed the harsh truth of a system rooted in injustice and inequality.

The Early Years: Deceiving Strength

Gold reserves gave South Africa's Rand deceptive early strength despite underlying economic issues. The entrenched economic inequality remained hidden but ongoing beneath the surface.

The 1970s: Sanctions and Pressure Begin

The growing global disapproval of apartheid led to effective sanctions that started to affect South Africa. Economic sanctions together with the 1973 oil crisis put substantial pressure on the Rand which led to its depreciation.

The 1980s: The Rand Under Siege

South Africa faced a period of significant upheaval throughout the 1980s. The growing anti-apartheid movement heightened political instability which led to the Rand suffering from the resulting chaos. As investors pulled back their funds capital flight ensued which resulted in the currency losing significant value.

The declaration of a state of emergency in 1985 led to the Rand's value dropping below two Rands per US dollar which clearly demonstrated the economic crisis. Sanctions from the global community increased while South Africa faced greater isolation along with its struggling currency.

The Late 1980s: Glimmers of Hope, Economic Pain

Political negotiations between the government and the African National Congress (ANC) began at the end of the decade which signaled a glimmer of hope. Economic fragility persisted amid soaring inflation rates and widespread unemployment that disproportionately affected Black South African communities.

1990-1994: The Transition Begins

The freeing of Nelson Mandela and the legal recognition of the ANC in 1990 represented a transformative period in South African history. The shift towards democracy commenced while facing political unrest and unpredictable circumstances. The Rand, reflecting this precariousness, remained volatile.

1994: The Rand entered a new era during the emergence of democracy in South Africa.

In 1994 South Africa held its first democratic elections which resulted in Nelson Mandela becoming the president. As apartheid fell to history the world rejoiced while the Rand appeared to exhale with relief. The nation faced colossal rebuilding challenges while foreign investment slowly started to return.

The Post-Apartheid Era: Rebuilding and Rebalancing

Coming into power the new democratic government had to tackle the massive challenge of correcting historical injustices while developing employment opportunities and promoting economic expansion. The Rand served as an indicator for the country's advancement.

The Late 1990s: Global Pressures and the Asian Crisis

The late 1990s brought new challenges. Emerging markets such as South Africa suffered consequences when the Asian financial crisis from 1997 to 1998 spread its impact throughout the region. The Rand suffered considerable depreciation because investors moved their capital to safer assets.

The Early 2000s: Commodity Boom and a Stronger Rand

South Africa's resource-heavy economy benefited from the global commodity boom that occurred during the early 2000s. During a time of economic growth and stability the Rand showed strength.

2008: The Global Financial Crisis Strikes

The 2008 global financial crisis created massive disruptions throughout the world economy. Investors moved their money to safer assets which led to a severe weakening of the Rand during South Africa's experience of the global financial crisis.

The 2010s: A Decade of Volatility

The Rand experienced significant turbulence throughout the 2010s because of domestic political issues, international economic challenges, and credit rating reductions. Jacob Zuma's presidency from 2009 to 2018 severely damaged South Africa's economic stability through pervasive corruption allegations and state capture which undermined investor confidence and increased Rand volatility.

2018: Ramaphosa Takes Over, Hopes for Reform

The 2018 presidential transition to Cyril Ramaphosa produced an optimistic outlook for South Africa. The Rand experienced a temporary surge due to his reform promises and anti-corruption stance but fundamental economic problems continued to exist.

2020: The COVID-19 Pandemic Hits

South Africa suffered economic damage during the COVID-19 pandemic along with the rest of the world. The Rand reached its lowest value ever against the US dollar demonstrating the weakness of the South African economy.

2021-2023: Recovery and Resilience, But Challenges Remain

Despite the pandemic's impact the South African economy showed resilience while the Rand experienced some stabilization. Despite economic recovery efforts, the currency remained under pressure because of ongoing high unemployment rates along with continuous inequality and frequent power outages.

2024: An Election Year, Uncertainty Looms

The year 2024's election season caused fresh uncertainty because investors worried about the result's influence on both the economy and the Rand.

2025: The trajectory of the Rand serves as a barometer for South Africa's national progression.

The Rand's future remains uncertain as early 2025 shows how closely it stays connected to South Africa's fortunes. The currency's path will be determined by South Africa's political stability, economic reforms along with global economic conditions and how it handles critical problems such as corruption unemployment and power shortages.

South Africa's ongoing journey towards equality and prosperity demonstrates the resilience of the Rand. The currency's rise and fall reveals a nation's enduring spirit through its stories of struggle and hope.

Apartheid was a brutal racial separation system that led to intense suffering in South Africa but was eventually opposed through economic sanctions which affected the South African Rand (ZAR).

South Africa endured massive suffering under apartheid which established a brutal system of racial segregation and discrimination. Global powers implemented economic sanctions as an effective measure to undermine the apartheid system in South Africa. The South African Rand (ZAR) functioned as an essential gauge for governmental pressure while aiding the liberation movement.

Economic sanctions against South Africa caused notable effects on both the national economy and the value of the Rand currency.

The combination of trade restrictions with financial limitations and cultural boycotts formed the core of international sanctions that strengthened from the 1960s through the 1980s. The economic sanctions imposed on South Africa resulted in shrinking foreign investment inflows, international isolation and forced exit of companies that refused to support apartheid.

Investor concerns and decreased confidence about South Africa's future led to a decline in the Rand's value. A depreciated Rand increased import costs which drove inflation higher and worsened living conditions particularly for black South Africans who endured severe hardships during the apartheid era. The Rand continued to decline despite government attempts to manage the situation through exchange controls.

Financial stress played a critical role in diminishing the apartheid government's operational capacity and their control resources while making the oppressive system harder to maintain.

The Rand became an emblematic representation of the Anti-Apartheid Movement's progress.

As the Rand's value decreased it represented the fragility of apartheid demonstrating to international observers that the oppressive regime could not endure. Activists pointed to the Rand's declining strength to demonstrate their progress and advocated for harsher sanctions to amplify pressure on the government.

The economic difficulties South Africa faced from sanctions proved to be multifaceted. The economic pain felt by everyday citizens became bearable for many because they understood it as a required step toward achieving freedom. The anti-apartheid movement engaged in economic confrontation through boycotts and disinvestment calls while using economic pressure as a strategic tool.

The international community joined the fight against apartheid through anti-apartheid organizations that campaigned, pressured governments, and pushed companies to sever all ties with South Africa.

Economic Reconstruction After Apartheid: The Challenges

When Nelson Mandela became president in 1994 and apartheid ended South Africa encountered significant problems including the need for economic reconstruction. Sanctions yielded contradictory results because they contributed to ending apartheid while simultaneously harming the economy.

The post-apartheid government was tasked with restoring public trust and needed to secure foreign investment while generating employment opportunities and tackling severe socioeconomic inequality. The Rand faced continuous vulnerability because of both international market dynamics and national policy decisions. The transition was not easy.

The government implemented fiscal discipline to control spending and keep inflation low while pursuing a stable economic environment. While the economy resumed growth and foreign investment reappeared the progress rate was sluggish and numerous challenges persisted.

Persistent unemployment alongside poverty and inequality continued to afflict society deeply. The remnants of apartheid affected the economy because skills shortages and educational disparities prevented many black South Africans from securing quality jobs.

An examination of the Rand throughout the 21st Century while anticipating its state by 2025.

Since 1994, the Rand has demonstrated volatility due to global economic crises and domestic political turmoil alongside corruption both of which drove away investors and weakened confidence in the currency. The COVID-19 pandemic severely affected South Africa by leading to economic decline and depreciation of the Rand.

The Rand's direction in 2025 remains unclear and will depend on how both global economic circumstances and internal political decisions unfold. To enhance productivity and job creation while boosting economic competitiveness the government must tackle corruption and governance issues and build a business-friendly environment and education and infrastructure development.

The fight against inequality stands as a fundamental goal because it functions both as an ethical responsibility and an essential requirement for societal stability and economic health. Economic challenges and achievements will be mirrored in the Rand's value since a strong and stable Rand demonstrates a healthy economy.

The battle against historical economic challenges will demand sustained effort and time. South Africa battles economically while its government works to sustain the Rand's strength as a crucial element for national stability.

The economic data tells tales of human beings who show resilience through their struggles while maintaining their hopes. The Johannesburg street vendor experiences day-to-day consequences from the Rand's volatility because a weaker Rand causes prices to rise and profits to decline while making life more difficult. Global economic changes cause the Durban factory worker to fear job loss while they hope for future job security. The Cape Town student envisions education as their pathway to a better future while aspiring to build a prosperous South Africa through their contributions.

The Rand's condition impacts millions of South Africans and their daily lives demonstrate this connection. Human dignity drove the struggle against apartheid while today's economic struggles aim to establish justice and fairness in society.

South Africans have demonstrated tremendous resilience by moving past significant challenges as they persistently work toward creating a brighter future. Their stories are a source of inspiration. The Rand stands as an emblem representing people's battles and their pursuit of a better tomorrow.

The path ahead for the Rand and South Africa's economy remains unclear yet the resilient spirit of its people propels them toward a hopeful future. The Rand serves as a vital instrument for South Africans who are fighting to strengthen their economy with the ultimate goal of achieving a better standard of living.

The people possess great strength and refuse to surrender their fight. The Rand plays a crucial role in trade while representing a multifaceted national story. South Africa is making great efforts to address its challenges while promising a bright future.

Visualize the Rand as the commanding lion that rules over the African savanna. South Africa's potential and its challenges surface as the Rand roars throughout the global economy.

The Rand remains bound to the unpredictable nature of global commodity market fluctuations. The lion reaches its peak strength with a powerful roar during sunny days when grasslands flourish with greenery. The lion becomes restless and expresses its uncertainty through rumbling roars when drought hits and prey becomes scarce.

The Rand is a currency whose trajectory depends heavily on the market performance of gold, platinum, and diamonds. As precious commodity values climb high the Rand becomes stronger which draws investors and boosts economic growth in South Africa. The Rand weakens whenever commodity prices decline which results in economic vulnerability.

The Rand operates in a perilous environment much like a lion traversing dangerous terrain that presents continuous obstacles. The Rand frequently seeks stability during times of global economic disturbance alongside political upheaval and speculative threats.

The South African Reserve Bank acts as the vigilant protector of the Rand while working to keep stability. The bank manages interest rates through a system of rewards and restrictions similar to how an animal trainer guides their charges to control the Rand's movements. The South African Reserve Bank strategically uses its foreign currency reserves to intervene when needed to protect the Rand's value.

Business entities have developed strategies to cope with the Rand's volatile fluctuations. Businesses protect themselves against unexpected currency fluctuations through financial instruments like hedging which operates similarly to how a seasoned safari guide predicts and prepares for wild dangers.

The tale of the Rand goes beyond simple survival. It's also about ambition. South Africa envisions an African economic union where the Rand emerges as the leading force propelling regional prosperity.

Though this vision remains important its path is filled with various obstacles. African nations face economic disparities and political complexities and need strong institutions before a pan-African currency becomes feasible.

The outlook for the Rand up to 2025 contains many unknowns and promises an exciting narrative yet to unfold. The Rand must decide whether to remain bound to the unpredictable commodities market or discover new foundations for its power. The Rand must successfully navigate its volatile environment to establish itself as an embodiment of regional stability and leadership.

Only time will tell. But one thing is certain: South Africa's Rand illustrates a compelling narrative that demonstrates the nation's resilience and goals while highlighting its role in international markets.

The Rand faces an unknown future yet holds potential for improvement. Addressing inequality is key. Promoting inclusive growth is crucial. The digital Rand could serve as a major factor in economic transformation.

South Africa has the potential to create a future that benefits everyone through inclusive prosperity. A more stable Rand with increased strength can be achieved. It requires commitment and collaboration. It requires a focus on long-term solutions. Significant obstacles exist yet better possibilities are available. The journey is not easy. But the destination is worth striving for.

Envision a South Africa where its people's dynamic spirit finds its reflection in an economically flourishing nation. The Rand represents both societal advancement and mutual wealth in an envisioned prosperous future. In this future, the healing of deep inequality has created a new environment where opportunity reaches every individual.

This transformation hinges on a fundamental shift. This transformation requires South Africa to reject exclusive growth models and adopt inclusive economic strategies that provide equal opportunity for every citizen to succeed. Investments must focus on supporting people instead of exclusively chasing profits. A country's real value stems from its citizens' potential.

The digital Rand stands as an essential instrument throughout this transformative journey. This financial instrument acts as a bridge for marginalized people to access the formal economy while serving as a gateway for financial empowerment. A young entrepreneur in a rural village utilizes her mobile phone to obtain credit which helps expand her business and enables her to work towards her dreams. The digital Rand represents an economic promise by providing universal access to currency functionality.

The journey to this future contains several significant barriers. We need to connect everyone to digital tools so no one is excluded from the benefits of the digital revolution. Protecting cybersecurity and privacy needs to be our top priority because they maintain the confidence essential for this new financial environment.

The government needs to establish a stable and supportive environment which enables businesses to prosper. The goal should be to promote innovation instead of obstructing it with excessive bureaucracy. The future demands investment in education and skill development to prepare younger generations for the dynamic challenges and opportunities that lie ahead.

This responsibility extends beyond government responsibility alone. The achievement of this goal relies on the active engagement of every South African citizen. Local businesses require support while better government performance needs to be demanded in addition to exploring digital economy opportunities.

The journey ahead is not easy. But the rewards are immense. The strength of the Rand directly leads to South Africa becoming a nation where each citizen can access improved living conditions. This vision of the future requires our commitment because it deserves our faith.

The Israeli New Shekel: A Currency of Innovation, Resilience, and Geopolitical Challenges

From Rags to Riches: The Israeli Shekel's Incredible Journey

The Israeli Lira existed as the currency of the biblical land known for both milk and honey. The Israeli Lira existed as a frail currency that faced an ongoing struggle against the destructive force of hyperinflation. The prices skyrocketed with the speed of falafel sales during Friday evenings while people watched their savings disappear like hookah smoke.

The Israeli Lira started facing significant problems during the initial years following Israel's independence. The young nation faced a multitude of challenges: The early years of Israel's independence saw a nation fighting wars and absorbing large-scale immigration while undertaking the enormous challenge of building the country entirely from the ground up. The government responded to its desperate situation by printing lira at an unprecedented rate.

This action served only to intensify the ongoing inflation problem. The inflation rate skyrocketed to extreme levels with annual increases hitting 400%. Before their money lost value people spent it on everything they could find. The nation faced economic turmoil while its currency approached total failure.

Desperate times called for drastic measures. The government undertook a bold rescue initiative called the Economic Stabilization Plan in 1985. Like a skilled surgeon, they cut spending, raised taxes, and introduced a brand new currency: the New Israeli Shekel (NIS).

As a phoenix rises from ruins to life anew, so did the shekel emerge powerful after its destruction. The shekel possessed strength and stability and showed determination to escape the trap of hyperinflation. The government committed to maintaining strict control of the money supply while granting the Bank of Israel autonomous power to guide the shekel into promising times ahead.

The recovery process encountered multiple obstacles along its path. Economic shocks occurred while political pressures mounted and there were moments when fiscal discipline became difficult to maintain. The shekel proved its robustness by surviving through numerous challenges.

The shekel stands out as a leading currency in today's global market. The shekel's ability to trade freely showcases Israel's strong economic position and its advanced technological capabilities. The Bank of Israel maintains steady control over the shekel by applying inflation targeting and additional strategies to ensure its stability.

The enduring strength of the shekel demonstrates how national resilience and effective economic strategies enable countries to triumph over severe obstacles. This narrative provides hope by showing that a path exists even during the darkest periods.

The Shekel, Tech, and the World: A Balancing Act (2025 and Beyond)

Despite Israel's small geographical size its significant role in the global economy stems from its rapidly expanding technology sector. The Israeli Shekel (ILS) holds a vital position in the narrative alongside a complex relationship.

The Israeli Shekel maintained a strong position throughout recent years demonstrating exceptional strength at times. The strength of the Israeli Shekel allows travelers from Israel to maximize their overseas spending power. The strong Shekel creates significant obstacles for businesses which particularly affects tech companies.

The power of the Shekel affects Israel's tech industry in significant ways.

Think of Israeli tech companies as exporters. Their worldwide sales of software products and cybersecurity solutions along with other innovations generate income primarily in US dollars or Euros.

Israeli companies receive less Shekel revenue when the Shekel remains strong since dollars and Euros convert to fewer Shekels which also makes their products costlier for international buyers.

Running with ankle weights slows you down as much as a strong Shekel can hinder Israeli tech companies. Israeli tech leads with innovation but faces competitive challenges when the Shekel maintains high strength.

The "Start-Up Nation" and Global Connections

Israel receives the nickname "Start-Up Nation" because of its high density of startups relative to its population. The region operates as a dynamic center for innovation that brings substantial foreign investment.

International capital flows into Israeli enterprises to boost their growth and generate new employment opportunities. The currency gains strength when demand for Shekels rises.

Israel functions as a key player in the global economy where it exports technology products and draws skilled professionals while establishing partnerships with international organizations.

The rising value of the Shekel increases hiring costs for international experts and complicates global partnerships because Israeli goods and services become more expensive.

The Bank of Israel's Tightrope Walk

The Bank of Israel has a tough job: The Bank of Israel works to maintain economic stability while managing inflation rates and monitoring the Shekel's exchange value.

The Bank of Israel uses market interventions to purchase foreign currency with the aim of devaluing the Shekel. Excessive intervention by the Bank of Israel in the foreign exchange market produces massive foreign currency reserves which then generate their own set of challenges. It's a constant balancing act.

The Human Element: Beyond the Numbers

This is about people's lives: Israel's tech sector prospers because of the work done by its engineers, entrepreneurs, and researchers.

When the Shekel remains strong it becomes more difficult for companies to maintain competitive salary offers which could drive talented Israeli workers to seek employment overseas.

It also affects everyday Israelis. While a strong Shekel makes imported goods cheaper, economic problems in the tech sector affect all Israelis. Everyone needs both job security and economic growth.

Looking Ahead: 2025 and Beyond

Israel's economic fundamentals along with tech sector expansion will maintain Shekel's relative strength.

Israel faces the challenge of managing the negative consequences of a strong currency which will require innovative business strategies and government policy interventions.

Possible Strategies and Adaptations

Hedging: Businesses are able to utilize financial tools to "hedge" against exchange rate changes which helps provide protection and enables more precise forecasting of costs and revenues.
Diversification: Israeli businesses should target markets with favorable exchange rates and seek out partnerships across various regions.
Government Support: The Israeli government can help businesses deal with Shekel appreciation by providing tax relief and research development subsidies as incentives.
Increased Productivity: The most effective long-term solution involves achieving higher levels of innovation. Israeli businesses that produce distinct and beneficial products can remain competitive in the market even if their currency remains strong.

Focus on Value, Not Price: Israeli companies now focus on their product quality and uniqueness to compete based on value rather than price levels.

The Human Factor: Adapting and Innovating

The resilience and boldness known as "chutzpah" displayed by Israeli entrepreneurs enables them to think creatively and embrace risk-taking. Despite the strength of their currency, Israeli businesses develop strategies to surpass this challenge.

Global Integration: A Two-Way Street

The economic integration of Israel extends beyond exporting products to include the importation of ideas as well as talent and capital from international markets. The strength of the Shekel helps Israel better attract international investors and facilitates the purchase of foreign businesses which enhances their global market standing.

The Delicate Dance Continues

The Shekel's connection to the tech sector and global integration will persist as a complex issue. There's no easy answer or magic formula.

The Bank of Israel will keep a close watch on developments and will adjust its policies as necessary to achieve balance. Israeli companies will persist in adapting their practices and creating innovative solutions while utilizing their competitive advantages.

The future is uncertain, but one thing is clear: The Shekel will play an essential role as Israel's tech sector maintains its status as a global economic powerhouse. The objective should be to enable the Shekel to fulfill a beneficial role instead of becoming an obstacle.

Global observers draw inspiration from Israel's economic achievements and apply its lessons throughout diverse contexts.

The Israeli Shekel: The Israeli Shekel represents more than economic value in a region marked by ongoing conflict (2025).

A coin worn smooth from years of circulation exchanges hands among people in a busy marketplace. The Israeli Shekel (ILS) stands for more than currency as it represents both resilience and struggle while playing a critical role in Israel's economic and political narrative.

The Arab-Israeli conflict creates significant influence over the Israeli Shekel's stability and value. The Arab-Israeli conflict has determined the Israeli Shekel's path by affecting its value and deeply influencing Israel's economic landscape.

The Weight of Conflict:

Guns and Butter: Israel faces significant financial pressure from defense expenditures which remain unavoidable due to permanent regional tensions. Money spent on military equipment for tanks and fighter jets represents funds unavailable for building educational schools and healthcare facilities.
Fear and Hesitation: Uncertainty is the enemy of investment. Foreign as well as domestic businesses show reluctance to invest money in regions where conflict could break out suddenly.
Tourism's Rollercoaster: Tourism potential exists in the Holy Land yet ongoing conflicts often halt its progress. Empty

hotels and dusty restaurants reflect the shekel's economic strain.
The Human Cost: The true cost of the conflict includes factors beyond financial amounts measured in shekels. Military service disrupts workers while families face destruction and lives come to an end.
Trade Winds and Blockades: When borders transform into walls trade routes evolve into dead ends the shekel faces obstacles in its movement. Boycotts increase economic pressure on Israel which simultaneously discovers new international trading partners.
Inflation's Bite: Conflict breeds instability, and instability fuels inflation. The shekel loses its purchasing power which results in higher everyday expenses.
Tech Sector in the Crosshairs: Even Israel's thriving tech sector isn't immune. Israeli tech companies face planning difficulties because reserve duty summons skilled engineers and ongoing uncertainty pushes project timelines back.
The World's Pressure: Economic pressures from sanctions combined with international criticism have created additional financial burdens which affect the shekel's performance and its position in the global financial markets.

The Shekel's Dance:

Volatility's Grip: Conflict escalation makes the shekel mirror the same level of unpredictability. Investors transfer their funds to the US dollar to secure their investments during turbulent times which leaves the shekel exposed to economic challenges.
Resilience in the Face of Adversity: Nevertheless, the shekel demonstrates remarkable durability in surviving economic pressures. The robust economy of Israel benefits from its cutting-edge technology industry which enables quick recovery from economic obstacles.

The Central Bank's Balancing Act: The Bank of Israel functions as a protector of the shekel through its strategic buying and selling activities to ensure stable value and prevent extreme fluctuations.
Reserves as a Shield: Israel keeps foreign exchange reserves to act as protection from economic disturbances.
More Than Just Numbers: The value of the shekel reflects Israel's national pride. When the shekel remains strong it strengthens national morale while its weakness generates widespread feelings of anxiety.

Cooperation's Hurdles:

Economic partnership between Israelis and Palestinians resembles negotiating a tightrope walk amidst a raging hurricane.

Walls and Checkpoints: The trade becomes a logistical nightmare as security concerns create movement barriers for goods and people.
Trust's Broken Bridge: Long-standing conflicts have destroyed trust which stands as a major obstacle in forming partnerships necessary for economic development.
Political Quicksand: The Palestinian Authority's instability prevents the creation of sustainable economic agreements.
An Uneven Playing Field: The dominant Israeli economy creates power imbalances that prevent effective cooperation with its Palestinian counterpart.
Settlements: Settlements in the West Bank by Israel create ongoing tension which obstructs economic collaborations while generating hostility.
Aid's Double-Edged Sword: International aid provides necessary support to sustain the Palestinian economy which simultaneously risks creating economic dependency.

Water: Survival depends on access to water yet competition for this vital resource intensifies existing tensions.
Gaza's Isolation: The Gaza blockade has devastated its economy and forced its residents into poverty and despair.

The Shekel's Regional Role:

A Currency Shared and Contested: The shekel functions as currency within Palestinian territories which shows the interconnected nature of regional economic systems. The Palestinian Authority aspires to establish its own currency which represents independence.
Peace's Economic Promises: Economic provisions have become standard components of peace agreements because trade and financial partnerships play a key role in maintaining peace.
Regional Integration: A Distant Dream? A regional currency like the "New Shekel" exists only as a distant possibility until the current conflict reaches resolution.
New Doors Opening: The Abraham Accords have opened new trade and investment channels which may strengthen the shekel and enhance economic connections throughout the region.
The Digital Frontier: The introduction of a digital shekel by Israel stands to revolutionize regional commerce by streamlining transactions while introducing fresh complexities.

The Road Ahead:

Uncertainty's Long Shadow: The ongoing conflict maintains a complex relationship with the shekel's future and regional economic development.
Can Economics Lead to Peace? There are two perspectives where some people believe economic

collaboration fosters political resolutions but others maintain peace should be established before economic initiatives can succeed.
Technology's Double-Edged Sword: Technology serves as an engine for progress by enabling trade and building opportunities yet poses risks because it may be used for surveillance and control purposes.
Climate Change: The region faces additional tension as water scarcity together with other climate-related challenges could lead to more conflict.
Global Economic Tides: International economic trends will have a significant impact on the shekel and regional economy through varying factors such as inflation and energy prices.

The shekel represents more than a financial medium because it reflects the region's aspirations along with its challenges and instability. The outcome of the shekel depends on global economic shifts alongside human perseverance and peace efforts.

The Israeli Shekel: A Journey into the Unknown

Envision the shekel as more than physical money but as a main character within an epic tale. The narrative encompasses innovative breakthroughs alongside regional aspirations and enduring efforts to achieve peace.

The shekel stands at a pivotal moment as it confronts the emergence of digital currency. Picture a reality where your shekels appear as radiant numbers on your phone screen and move between accounts instantly with just a tap. The digital shekel stands as a transformative force which may revolutionize Israel's financial environment.

Think of the possibilities: The digital shekel will enable quick transactions while reducing fees and providing access to advanced financial technology. Every hero's journey includes obstacles that must be conquered. Digital cybersecurity threats hide in the background while public confidence remains crucial to establish. Through meticulous management of existing challenges the Bank of Israel guarantees the digital shekel becomes a positive influence.

The narrative of the shekel stretches across international boundaries. A Middle East exists where economic integration replaces old conflicts with mutual prosperity. The shekel stands to serve as a conduit uniting businesses while providing momentum to startup growth and enabling cross-industry partnerships in technology and sustainable resource management.

This vision faces formidable obstacles: Political instability combined with deep-seated mistrust and the persistent Israeli-Palestinian conflict stands as a major barrier. Yet, the potential rewards are immense. Visualize a region where economic partnerships create enduring peace and currencies including the shekel move freely to unite nations together.

The path of the shekel stands as a mirror to Israel's ongoing pursuit of both peace and prosperity. This pursuit requires bravery alongside steadfast determination and openness to novel opportunities. The younger generations who dream of a better tomorrow provide essential momentum for this endeavor.

The shekel exists beyond its monetary function through its physical and digital representations. The shekel represents Israel's economic strength while functioning as an instrument for advancement and a possible driver for regional change. The fate of this entity remains connected to what will happen to the region as they move together in an uncertain yet hopeful balance.

The narrative of the shekel continues to unfold. This narrative unfolds through a journey of dreams and obstacles while showcasing the relentless spirit of mankind. This narrative encourages us to envision a future in which both the shekel and its people will flourish.

About Author

Azhar ul Haque Sario is a bestselling author and data scientist with a remarkable record of achievement. This Cambridge alumnus brings a wealth of knowledge to his work, holding an MBA, ACCA (Knowledge Level - FTMS College Malaysia), BBA, and several Google certifications, including specializations in Google Data Analytics, Google Digital Marketing & E-commerce, and Google Project Management.

With ten years of business experience, Azhar combines practical expertise with his impressive academic background to craft insightful books. His prolific writing has resulted in an astounding 2810 published titles, earning him the record for the maximum Kindle editions and paperback books published by an individual author in one year, awarded by Asia Books of Records in 2024.

ORCID: https://orcid.org/0009-0004-8629-830X
Azhar.sario@hotmail.co.uk
https://www.linkedin.com/in/azharulhaquesario/

www.ingramcontent.com/pod-product-compliance
Lightning Source LLC
Chambersburg PA
CBHW031349230926
51848CB00002B/451
9783384629388